LOVING AGAINST THE ODDS

Loving Against the Odds

Rob Parsons

Hodder & Stoughton
LONDON SYDNEY AUCKLAND

Copyright © 1994 by CARE TRUST
First published in Great Britain in 1994
by Hodder and Stoughton, a division
of Hodder Headline PLC

20 19 18 17 16 15 14 13 12 11

A CIP Catalogue record for this title is available from the
British Library

ISBN 0 340 61074 3 Hbk
0 340 59315 6 Pbk

Printed and bound in Great Britain by
Cox & Wyman Ltd, Reading, Berkshire

Hodder and Stoughton
A division of Hodder Headline PLC
338 Euston Road
London NW1 3BH

Dedication

To my wife Dianne
To my children Katie and Lloyd
To Ron who has become a brother
To our friends at Glenwood Church Centre -- all of whom
have loved me -- against the odds

Contents

	Acknowledgements	9
	Foreword	11
	Introduction	13
1.	Love in the Real World	17
2.	Whatever Happened to Conversation?	24
3.	Time for Love	34
4.	A Word to Fathers	47
5.	Hey – Look Who's Talking!	60
6.	How to Fight a Good Fight	75
7.	Rain in the Desert – The Power of Appreciation	96
8.	Rediscovering Sex	118
9.	Fatal Attraction	140
10.	The Heart of the Affair	152
11.	Dealing with the Past – The Freedom of Forgiveness	170
12.	Till Debt us do Part	183
13.	Loving Against the Odds	201
	Notes	219

Acknowledgements

A number of friends have given help in forming and editing material for this book. Grateful thanks to Jim Boston, Jacqui Butler, Gareth Crossley, Jane Lawry, Paul McCusker, Keith Tondeur, and to all the staff at CARE for the Family, especially Sheron Rice, Maureen Erny, June Way and Gaynor Deans. Special thanks to James Catford, my editor, and to Edward England, my agent.

There is nobody in the whole family arena that I respect more than Dr James Dobson. He has encouraged me more than he will ever know. At CARE for the Family we count him and his staff among our closest allies.

God has given to me in Lyndon Bowring, Charlie Colchester and Jonathan Booth three special friends who have become like brothers. I am so grateful for them and to them.

This is a book based on real-life events. Whenever situations or letters are quoted, names and some facts have been altered to preserve anonymity. If original letters are published, then permission has been sought and granted, although even there, names, and some facts, have been changed.

Foreword

We were first introduced to Rob and Dianne Parsons when our church showed the film of their 'Marriage Matters' seminar. We have never been to an event like it! The three hours went in a moment. Here at last were people tackling, honestly, the issues that affect every marriage – but with an admission that they were fellow sufferers! The audience were spellbound. One minute there was helpless laughter as Rob talked about some of the crazy expectations we often have of each other or the way we row over the silliest things, the next an occasional tear as Dianne talked about deep lessons learnt from a time of protracted illness.

We are thrilled that Rob has taken the heart of *Marriage Matters* and given us *Loving Against the Odds*. As we read it we saw not only the lessons we had seen on screen expanded, but masses of new material. It is destined to become a major resource to families in this country.

The key to the book is that it is *real*. Rob has the knack not only of identifying the problems and joys of marriage, but of identifying *with them*. He talks about the rows he and Dianne have had, their disappointments, and even times when they did not 'feel' in love. But it's not just an honest book, it's a book filled with hope and compassion – with understanding – and with *practical* down-to-earth help bursting out of every chapter.

We recommend this book to you if you've got a fantastic marriage – it will help to protect it. We would urge you to read it if you are engaged or newly-wed, and even if it seems that your love has died, you may well find, as many have in Rob's seminars, that there can be hope of finding love again – even against the odds.

Roy and Fiona Castle

Introduction

A top-security space station is a strange setting for a marriage seminar! I had been invited to Moscow to address psychiatrists, doctors, social workers and military personnel on family issues. One of the seminars was held in 'Space City', the location from which the Russians run their space programme. It was from here that Yuri Gagarin began his momentous journey in 1961.

As I spoke, I wondered how well the seminar was translating, and began to dread the pending question time. Would these people from such a different culture have questions that I had never heard before? I finished speaking, and the chairman opened the seminar to the audience. A woman in her mid-forties raised her hand and then gave her question. I sat on the edge of my seat as he translated it for me: 'My husband doesn't communicate with me. How can I get him to talk?' I couldn't help but smile. We were two thousand miles from home and hearing the most common question we get asked in the United Kingdom! Perhaps some things really are the same the world over!

Whether we live in Manchester or Moscow, our relationships have the potential for incredible happiness and unbelievable pain. We have had the privilege of presenting our CARE for the Family seminars, live, to over fifty thousand people in several different countries, and to many thousands of others by video. I am grateful for that, because in them we set out, before all else, to let people know that they are not alone. So many of us who are going through difficult times do so believing that this is 'just us'.

Once we have broken that sense of isolation, it's easier to go on to find solutions. We all need help. Whether we have a strong marriage or feel that love has died, we were never meant to make it on our own. This book was born out of those seminars, and although it contains a great deal of new material, the heart is the same.

In some of our seminars Dianne is able to speak with me, but in others, because of family responsibilities, that is not possible. *Loving Against the Odds* is a little like that. I wrote it, but in every other sense it is *our* book.

Just as a wide variety of people attend our seminars, so there will be differences in those who read this book. Some will be in the middle of some deep trauma, perhaps going through a time when their marriage seems dry and lifeless. There will be those whose marriages are strong and who, wisely, want to do all they can to protect their relationship. There will be single people who may intend to be married, and those who have known the pain of divorce. I mention children, but I know that, for a variety of reasons, some who read the book will not have children of their own. At times I will share a little of the faith that I have come to believe, and yet I know that there will be people of other faiths, and no faith, who will read this book. Please be patient with me.

What I can promise you is that I have tried to be as honest and realistic as possible. The last thing most of us need is for somebody to give us a handful of easy answers, or to give the impression that if we had a marriage like theirs life would be perfect.

Let me introduce our family to you. Dianne and I have been married for almost twenty-three years. We have two teenage children, Katie and Lloyd. We also have a very special member of our family. Some years ago Ron, who is forty-eight, was practically living rough and came to live with us. He has been with us longer than the children!

So let's begin. We will laugh together, and perhaps even cry a little. But this is an incredible journey; for the older we get and the more clearly we understand ourselves, the more we realise that the greatest thing in life is to find somebody, somewhere, who will love us . . . against the odds.

1

Love in the Real World

When Lloyd, my son, was small, we would sometimes play chess together before he went to bed. He had only just learnt the moves, and I would normally sacrifice a few pieces in order to build his confidence. But some evenings, when I was really tired, I would do the equivalent of skipping pages when we read toddlers a bedtime story – I would pull out an old move. It was the one I used last week and the week before – pawn, queen, bishop, queen – checkmate! 'That was quick, dad,' he would say. 'Can we play again?' 'No, son,' I'd reply; 'I did say, "Just one game."' And I would leave his room a little shamefaced, knowing that the days when I could use that tired old move were numbered.

In our work in CARE for the Family, we watch marriages break up before our eyes. We see little children devastated by the break-up of their families. We see affairs that leave behind a trail of broken hearts, hopes and lives. And as I observe these things I see that time and time again it's the same old moves that wage war against the family – lack of communication, sexual difficulties in marriage, finance, taking each other for granted – and these are just a few.

I remember some years ago watching a television documentary on grouse shooting – it looked to me more like a turkey shoot! A beater was employed to go ahead of those shooting. It was his job to scare the birds into the air – and, sure enough, it worked. He hit the bracken and, as if

17

anxious to please, the birds flew up – bang! I felt like yelling to them, 'Stay down! Keep your heads low. It's the same old trick!' Yet we have allowed couples to walk into marriage without even the most basic preparation for what might lie ahead. We have given them no idea of the old strategies that may assault their relationship.

In our defence it may be said that we fell victim to the natural optimism that it's so easy to feel at the beginning of a relationship. We wanted to believe that love will triumph in the end. Part of the reason for that may have been a conviction that our family would never know such difficulties, or maybe we assumed that because this couple were members of our church, somehow they would be protected from the onslaught that others have faced.

We don't need convincing now. We all have friends who are going through the trauma of divorce, and many of us know Christian leaders whose marriages are going through difficult times. The sad thing is that so much of this has come as a surprise to us. We have fallen for the old ruses because the one ingredient that has been lacking more than any other is honesty.

We have imagined that the people in our circle were immune – that there were not couples all around us who did not feel in love, that there was nobody who could have been feeling that they couldn't spend another day with their partner. We have imagined that when people said, 'Oh, I'm fine,' they really meant it.

We have not only pretended that all is well with those around us, but have tried to wear the mask of perfection ourselves. One man, when announcing that our *Marriage Matters* seminar was coming to his town, said, 'Of course, my wife and I won't be there – we have no problems in that area.' That attitude is so often borne out of good intentions, but it is unreal and so very dangerous. It is dangerous for several reasons.

Firstly, we may fool others for a while, but eventually we

die inside. We find that the constant battle always to appear as though we are above all the traumas that hit others is utterly draining. Secondly, we help create a culture where others are condemned to pretend that they too are 'very well, thank you'.

So many of the marriages that have broken up around us have done so in isolation. These couples have believed that they have been the only ones who ever felt like this. Many of those who have fallen into affairs have done so honestly believing that there wasn't another man or woman on the planet who could genuinely understand, let alone possibly experience, what they were going through.

The sad thing about all this is that we were never meant to face such issues in isolation. God knows what we are feeling, and the Bible is so very honest about all its heroes. Yet so often we have missed the power that there is in weakness. Many of us seem to be so successful that nobody can get near to us. Our marriages seem to be so together in every way, our children never pick their noses in public, and we give the impression that the pains that hit others pass us by. But when we let a little of our weakness – failure even – show through, we allow others to share how they are feeling. Dianne and I have some first-hand experience of this, as we'll share later in the book, and we have noticed that whenever you say those wonderful words, 'Me, too,' you are so often greeted with first surprise and then sheer relief.

The truth is that all of us go through difficult periods in our family relationships. Nobody is immune from this. I believe that in almost every marriage there will come a period when at least one of the partners will not *feel* in love.

It is not at all uncommon for somebody to imagine the death of their spouse. They imagine getting the news that he or she has suddenly died. They begin to savour the freedom that they would then have, and often the exciting relationships that would develop with a new, often imaginary, person. When I say that during one of our seminars, perhaps in front of a thousand people, I first of all see looks of shock. A moment later, those looks change from shock to relief, and then almost imperceptibly to wry amusement. They are realising that after all they are not the only ones in the whole world who have felt that way.

Not until we face these issues openly and honestly is there any chance at all that we will be able to stem the tide of family break-up, let alone reverse it. For it is not until there is an acknowledgement of the problem that we become aware enough to stop the old enemies that conspire to kill love.

One enemy is time pressure. It may be a husband who seems so very busy. Life at work is frantic, and he is involved in many outside activities. He comes home late in the evening and sits down to a hurried meal before rushing off to another meeting. At that meal table he is silent, engrossed in the thoughts of the day and the events that lie ahead. This is a busy man. He is on many committees. If anything is to be done, you need to get this man involved. He is a brilliant counsellor, and has helped so many people. All that would be well, if it were not the case that his own family needs his counsel but cannot get it.

I find that this situation is often summed up in a letter something like this:

My husband is a real family man and totally dedicated to me and our three children. He has a lot of responsibility at our church and is so very busy there. I so much want us to do things together, but where is the time? I'd like us to go for a walk together – to have times when we hold hands and say 'I love you' – times without the kids there or even the need to make love. I love him dearly and I want no other – I know that I need to change, too, but I'm so frightened that when the children have flown the nest, there will be nothing left. We so rarely go to bed at the same time – I'm half asleep when he comes up.

20

Then, if he makes the effort to come up early, I know what he wants, rightly, and I can't. I feel used. I want him to spend time with me – not just for sex – a quick five minutes – but to walk and talk and not to watch TV. You see, I'm such a failure.

In another home, it may not be time pressure, but rather that a man feels that his wife is taking him for granted. She pulls him down in public and he is tired of the old jokes. He is forty-five years old and suddenly he feels trapped. It just seems that life is slipping by so quickly. His body is ageing and he fantasises about a new relationship – and then it happens: he feels himself drawn towards a woman at work. He flirts a little and then feels incredible shame. He wonders what life would be like with her. He needs to talk to somebody, but who could ever understand? And so he isolates himself – from wife, from friends – even from God. When he falls, it is both sudden and catastrophic.

We can do something about these situations. But to do this, we need honesty.

Dianne and I have been married for almost twenty-three years, and we have gone through some difficult periods in that time. We have known times when we have not felt in love, times when it seemed that love had almost died. The heart of our seminars and the essence of this book is not just to provide answers. I want to do that, of course; but just as much, I want to tell you that whatever your situation, whether it is incredible joy right now or unbelievable pain, it is not unique – others have walked and are walking that path. And many who thought that love had died have found it again – stronger than before.

Nobody who is going through a difficult time can believe that, but it is true. Dianne and I see the evidence of it week in, week out. Like the woman who wrote:

You may not remember me, but we talked with you about the problems in our marriage – they seemed to be getting steadily worse. It is only fair to let you know how things have developed since. The improvement that has occurred is, humanly speaking, impossible. This is not just a feeling – even the children have commented on it. Before, they knew that Simon loved them, but they have not known how to relate to him. Now their love for their dad is growing much stronger and is visible. The atmosphere in our home is relaxed. Peace rules – and that through all the hustle and bustle of daily life. This is the marriage that I dreamt of twenty years ago! I have wanted to tell you earlier, but somehow now it seems more real because it has stood the test of time.

One of the stories that I love to tell is about a man in a supermarket. The trolley he was pushing contained not only the week's provisions, but also a two-year-old child. The child was screaming, yelling and kicking, but the man was speaking softly in measured tones: 'Don't get upset, George, don't cry, George, don't scream, George.'

An old lady who was nearby felt that she must comment on this shining example of fatherhood. 'Sir,' she said, 'may I commend you on the way you are dealing with young George?' 'Madam,' he replied wearily, '*I'm* George!'

That is how so many of us feel. We just want to look to heaven and say, 'Lord, I'm George!'

If you have a marriage in which you never row, always feel in love, and find there's simply not enough time to fit in all the sex you both crave for, then I hope this book will make your love even stronger. But I have to confess, it was written for people like Dianne and myself, who love each other but have known times when the feeling of love did not come easily – times when it seemed that love had all but died. But then was born a determination to love – not because of, but in spite of the circumstances and how we felt. It was a resolve to love, not just with the heart, but with the will and the spirit. It was a refusal to let go easily of something that had been precious and was now a part not only of our lives, but the lives of others. It was, in short, a cry to heaven to rekindle love as it had been, only stronger; and it was a plea to bring that change about by teaching us how to do what heaven is good at – loving against the odds.

In *Loving Against the Odds*, I want us to look at the old moves that time and time again are causing marriages to fail, and at ways of strengthening our love. And therein lies a secret. The enemies of love are very old . . . but its friends are too.

2

Whatever Happened To Conversation?

When Di and I were engaged, we went for long walks together and dreamt of what it would be like when finally we were married. In those far off days, we would muse about a typical day in our future lives together. I would go out and work all day to provide for our basic needs – mortgage payments, television, egg whisk – and Di would also labour all day to provide those little extras, like food.

We would both rush home to capture as much time together as possible and argue over who had the privilege of doing the meal that night. 'You made the Duck à l'Orange last night – it's my turn.' That delightful banter would carry on until reluctantly, one of us would leave the kitchen, slide into warm slippers and await another culinary triumph. As we ate, we would discuss each other's day, and then our hopes and aspirations for the future together. Finally, as the coffee ambled through the percolator, we would debate great world issues and crack impossible theological dilemmas. In the evening, delightful friends would call and although we would enjoy their company, we would eventually firmly usher them out of the door as the prospect of bed, and therefore unbridled passion, beckoned.

We were not foolish enough to believe that all our evenings would be spent in such unsullied bliss, and were fully prepared for the shock if once a month it didn't quite turn out as we had planned.

We have now been married for over twenty-two years – that's twenty-two years of real living. If you asked Di and me whether we would prefer married life as we imagined it or as it is, we wouldn't even hesitate – give us the dreams every time! But none of us can have the dreams, and the truth is, although they seem alluring, we'd probably die of boredom. (Di says she'll risk the boredom – she'd still like to give the dreams a try!)

As we look back, we smile at the way untried love can imagine the future, and at its inability or unwillingness to look reality in the eye. And therein lies one of the great flaws of marriage-preparation classes. Before I go on, let me say clearly that I believe marriage preparation ought to be compulsory. If you have to have lessons to drive a car, taking a few to obtain a husband or a wife isn't so silly. But there is a major difficulty leaders of such groups have to face. In short, the couples don't believe you. You say to them, 'You may have difficulties in your sex life.' They look at you as if you've told a four-year-old he may have difficulty eating chocolate. You say, 'Keep the romantic fires alive.' Even as you speak, they are crawling over each other and nod sympathetically. But the real 'no winner' is when you tell them to keep talking to each other – never to get to the stage where those lines of communication dry up. I admit it is difficult for them to grasp the reality of this potential problem. When you can easily spend five hours discussing the wallpaper that you're going to have in the downstairs toilet, it's hard to believe that conversation could ever be difficult.

And yet those of us involved in marriage preparation, whether it's the homely advice of a parent or in classes at a local church, simply must raise this matter. And we must do it for one basic reason: of all the issues that can kill love in a marriage – conflict, the affair, financial trauma, sexual difficulty – lack of communication is without doubt not only in a class of its own, but at the heart of so many of the other difficulties.

We don't talk any more

If that lack of communication is left to grow, we see develop what someone has called 'a creeping separateness'.

I saw that 'separateness' so graphically illustrated some years ago. I was in a busy restaurant with a friend. There was a buzz of conversation about the place. In one corner sat a family laughing and joking, in another what seemed to be a works outing. As we stood and waited, I glanced around the room; and then I saw them. They were sitting at a far table, a man and woman in their mid-forties. They seemed almost immobile. He was gazing with unseeing eyes into the sports page of a newspaper, she sat watching him. They would occasionally speak, but when they did they looked as if they were discussing the weather. Who were they, these two who in this restaurant, humming with conversation, seemed so incongruous? My friend whispered in my ear, 'I bet they're married!' Whether he was right or not, we'll never know, and yet his very comment highlighted the lack of conversation that many have come to expect as normal in a marriage.

How they contrast with a couple Dianne and I came across the other night. We were in a dimly lit restaurant, enjoying a special night out. The room was full and the tables close together. Suddenly, a comment from the table behind made us realise that the couple were involved in an illicit meeting. We both stopped eating and I nearly broke my neck leaning backwards on the chair, trying to listen to the conversation. And it was conversation! They were talking in animated fashion, and one sensed that even passing the salt was an adventure. As we left, they were still talking, but the strange thing is, it wouldn't have mattered if they hadn't been. They were so obviously *with* each other, not just in sounds spoken, but in attention.

In our work in CARE for the Family we see too many affairs to be over-impressed with that scene. It's not difficult to have incredible conversation in the early months of an affair. And yet, in marriage, we must strive to hold on to the best of that and to foster the belief that we care enough about each other to speak . . . and to listen.

A marriage does not normally die overnight. It may be that an event such as an affair will suddenly cause the heart of love to die, but much more common is that week by week, month by month, year upon year, the couple simply grow apart. So often, by the time they reach out for help, for one of the partners at least, the marriage seems to be dead. He will say to us, 'I realise now that I probably never loved her.' She will whisper, 'I find even the sound of his voice irritates me.' But he did love her once, and there was a time when she loved to hear him speak. Yet somewhere along the road that love seems to have died. What has caused this?

So often, it is because this couple have simply stopped talking to each other. By that, I don't mean that they don't speak, but rather that there is no in-depth communication. They exchange facts – the children's progress at school, the cost of a new washing machine – but they have stopped letting each other know how they *feel*.

That is summed up so powerfully in the following letter:

Andy and I were so in love when we got married. It was nothing for us in those early days to sit and talk for hours. Even when we weren't speaking, there was a sense that we knew what the other was feeling. It's hard to know when we really grew apart. Andy's job became more and more demanding and I had the children to see to. It may have been that I gave them too much attention and he felt excluded, but, looking back, I honestly feel if I hadn't been speaking to them, I wouldn't have been talking to anybody. He came home so tired he could hardly say 'hello', let alone tell me about his day or even pretend to be interested in mine. I hated it. I longed to speak to him. Sometimes, after we had made love, I would for a moment believe he felt close to me and, as we lay there, I would begin to tell him so much of what I had been longing to say. But so often, as I shared my heart, I would realise that he was already asleep. And then a strange thing happened. I learnt to live without him. Oh, I washed his clothes and cooked and tried hard to be a wife to him, but inside I learnt to live apart from him. It was as if something inside me said, 'You're on your own – for your sake and the kids' sake, face it and learn to live with it.' And then I eventually realised that I didn't love him any more. The voice I had longed to hear I now hated. He must have sensed that because, incredibly, he then wanted to talk. But it was too late – it was over.

'You have no idea what it's like living with somebody you love who just won't communicate with you. In truth, it makes islands of you both.' Whenever Dianne and I have gone through difficult periods in our marriage, a symptom has been that so often we seemed to have no time or inclination to talk in depth to each other. Di would say to me, 'How come you can spend an hour on the phone to somebody from work and yet you find it so hard to talk to me for ten minutes? How can we be at a party and I'll hear you tell somebody of some new idea you've had, or some really important news, but you've not told me? How can that happen to you and me who have become one?'

My daughter Katie summed up the problem one evening. She was just four then, and had been trying to get my attention for an hour. Finally, she clambered on to a chair, looked straight up at my head and yelled, 'Is there anybody in there?'

From the letters that we receive, we realise that Dianne and Katie are not the only females who find it difficult to get the men in their lives talking to them.

It is a major complaint of women that men don't communicate. The following letter from June is typical:

> I don't know if I will have the courage to post this letter. Over the years, I have written many such, but never posted them. I have been married for twenty years, but now I have just left my husband. My husband is an island. Over all the years of our marriage, he would discuss *nothing* – from moving house to whether or not to take sandwiches or hot dogs on a picnic. He told me that he did not want to talk about his work, and over the years made it clear to me that almost everything was out of bounds for conversation – whether it was a film we had been to or an evening with friends. I realised that we were in big trouble. I bought books and was so excited because I found answers, but after ten years, I gave up – I was so frustrated. He just dismissed me.

She calls him 'an island', but the reality is even sadder than that. By his decision or inability to communicate, he actually made her an island as well. I have no doubt that she felt utterly isolated.

Dr Philip Zimbardo, Professor of Psychology at Stamford University, has said, 'I know of no more potent killer than isolation. There is no more destructive influence on physical and mental health than the isolation of you from me.'[1] Isolation so often occurs when both partners become absorbed with their own lives and feel unwilling or unable to share themselves in meaningful communication with their partner. Its devastating power lies in the fact that it destroys not only the one who feels excluded, but also the one who has withdrawn into him or herself.

The tragedy of June's story is that when her husband

arrived home one night to find her gone, I have no doubt that
he was both surprised and filled with remorse. He may have
had no idea how deeply his wife felt about this situation.
She said that he wouldn't even talk about the little things.
Those 'little things' are important. I'm not impressed when
I hear somebody say that they can't stand what they call
'small talk' with their partner. It's talk about the small
non-threatening issues that lays a foundation of good communication. The truth is that if we don't communicate about
the small issues, then the first thing to hit us is a major
trauma. A husband is staggered to find the note stuck to
the fridge door – she's gone. A wife is devastated when he
says he needs what he calls 'a little space for a while'. It
seems to have come out of the blue – but it rarely has.

When silence isn't golden

Sadly, most men do find it more difficult than most women
to communicate in depth. One study[2] has shown that men
are more likely to commit suicide than women, and a major
factor in this is that they find it so much harder than women
to talk about things that are bothering them.

On one occasion I was speaking to sixty men in church
leadership. They all knew each other. My subject was 'Openness and Honesty'. When I had finished a man stood, looked
at his colleagues, and asked, 'Which of you would admit any
personal weakness to anybody else in this room?' To a man
they said, 'Never.'

It's a wise woman who understands that her husband may
find it difficult to share his heart, and who tries to help him
in this. The bad news is that some research suggests that
the older men get, the worse they become at communicating.
Studies undertaken in the University of Pennsylvania show
that ageng men lose their brain functioning, especially their
verbal abilities, faster than women. A study of men and
women aged eighteen to eighty showed that deterioration of

the brain's left side (the side associated with languages and verbal reasoning) occurs two to three times faster in men.[3]

I am not sure how much credence to give to that, but I am sure that men communicate in a different way to women. A man will come home from a meeting and his wife will say, 'What happened, darling?' In answer, he'll read her the agenda! She'll say, 'No, tell me what really happened. What was *she* like, how did *he* behave this time?' – but at eleven thirty at night it's a lost cause. They both have such different attitudes to the information that needs to be communicated. That difference has been summed up succinctly, 'When a man speaks, he gives you a piece of his mind. When a woman speaks, she gives you a piece of her heart.'[4]

Men generally find it much easier to tell you what they 'do' rather than what they are feeling. The first question that a man will ask another man at a party is, 'What do you do?' So often, men see communication as problem-solving, and not to do with feelings.

It may be for this reason that in many counselling situations some wives will raise the frustration that when their husband has a problem, he tends to go into 'silent mode' for a week or so. In one case, David had heard that he might be made redundant. He became very quiet and withdrawn. His wife had suspected the nature of the problem, but didn't want to intrude. She waited for him to share his worries . . . and she waited. In the end, she exploded: 'Will you please tell me what's wrong? I have a right to know. You must face up to it!' She had assumed that the cause of his silence was that he was hiding from the issue. In fact, the opposite was true. Her husband had been brought up in a culture that gave the impression that men are meant to be 'macho'. They are meant to provide for their families and not bleat when they can't do that. A real man would sort this out – and he was trying to sort it out. Far from denying the situation, he was thinking about it every waking moment, trying to find a way out of this trauma. When he brought it to his wife, he wanted to be able to say, 'I've lost my job at the factory, but on Monday I start at the new car-works.'

That kind of attitude, whether found in a man or a woman, causes the person to cut themselves off from family and even friends while they think the difficulty through. They may be desperate to share their feelings, but ingrained is the belief that you don't wear your heart on your sleeve; that capable people sort out their own problems.

When David's wife understood what was going on, she found it so much easier to cope with. He was devastated when he realised that his silence, far from protecting her, was a greater problem to her than the job loss. He came to understand that each of the family members, including the children, had felt as if they were the cause of his silence, and each had felt guilty. Many a wife has spent hours going back over the events of the past days or even months in a vain attempt to pinpoint what it was she said or did to cause the situation that is casting such gloom over the home.

On other occasions, we have seen a wife who finds it hard to communicate, to share what she is really thinking, and she will give up trying to talk to her husband. She may find a substitute, perhaps a mother or, more often, a close female friend. These women will share the most intimate secrets of their marriages together. Sometimes friends are more sympathetic than partners, and it's not uncommon to hear in a marriage, 'My friends listen to me more than you.' These relationships with friends are precious, but comparisons with the married partner are false. The friends don't have to live with the result of their advice day in, day out; they don't have to deal with the 'other side' of the argument. They only have to listen and sympathise. Such relationships can sometimes make it harder for couples to rediscover good communication in their marriage. In fact, they become a substitute for in-depth conversation between a husband and wife. They work best when friends encourage each other to try to rebuild deep relationships with their husband or wife, and when they bend over backwards not just to sympathise, but also to bring a sense of realism and perspective.

We sometimes see one of the partners unable to communicate because they have been bruised over the years. It may be a wife who has tried to raise issues, but has been put down. He has said, 'How can you possibly be depressed? You've got two lovely children, you've got a nice house, you've got a vacuum cleaner. You've got me!'

Real communication is vital if relationships are to deepen and grow. It is necessary to avoid that 'creeping separateness' – and yet there are so many couples who have *never* known it. They returned from honeymoon all those years ago, the phone started to ring, there was the house to fix up, so many friends to invite around, and then the children came along. They will sometimes look at those children, now teenagers, and say, 'Where have the years gone? They've flown by.' What they do not yet realise is the void that is at the heart of their marriage. Life with the children, and the busyness of life, keeps them, even saves them, from thinking about their relationship. But the day may come when the children leave, and other activities stop, and they will sit in a room, look at each other, and say in their hearts, 'Who are you?'

The good news is that we can change. In fact, at least half of the battle is realising what's going on. The other day, I received a letter from a woman who had been at one of our seminars: 'We have been married for twenty-five years. The day after the seminar, we skipped church, went for a long walk, and began to unpack all those years.'

These changes can revolutionise our relationship; love can begin to grow again where it seemed to have died, but for most of us there will be battles to be fought along the way. And not least with that great enemy – time.

3

Time for Love

The other day I sat at my desk, having just finished reading a typical week's mail. There were stories full of joy and hope, of families struggling through whatever hard times had come their way. There were letters of encouragement – people who had been helped by a book, a seminar, a video. But there were also the tragic letters – those that had come from men and women whose lives had been broken. In those letters, there were so often recurring themes, like that of the husband or wife coming home to find that the family had left:

> I entered an empty house and wandered around the rooms – they were gone. They had asked me over and over again to give them time, but I had such a busy job and so many commitments. Yet all I wanted as I stood in that hollow house was them back again. I wanted to hear my child say, 'Will you play with me, now?' I wanted to say to them, 'Yes, of course I remembered Emma's birthday.' I wanted to pull the telephone that I had never been able to resist right out of its socket, and rip the famous appointments diary in a hundred pieces. I wanted to tell them, 'You all really mattered to me more than it all. Forgive me.' I just wanted to roll back the years and begin again.

These emotions are not uncommon. In fact, if one scans surveys that list the factors that contribute to the break-up of family life, somewhere near the top will be the scourge of an over-busy life.

Racing with the rats

I was in New York at an international conference, where the senior partner of a major law firm was outlining his strategy for a successful legal practice.

'We like our young lawyers to work an average of fifteen hours per day,' he said. 'We have bedrooms at the office, showers and kitchens, because we find that going home interrupts their rhythm.'

The chairman turned and said, 'But Larry, what about burn out?' The reply was devastating: 'No problem, Jack – if they burn out, we don't want them.'

Thousands of families all across our nation are burning out for exactly the same reason as those young lawyers – they are just too busy. When we are conducting one of our stress seminars, I ask the audience, 'How many of you own an electric iron?' Every hand goes up. 'How many have a washing machine?' – almost every hand. And then I say, 'I'll bet that some of you have an electric iron *and* a washing machine – you may even have a dishwasher and a hoover.' Then I ask, 'Did your grandmother have those time-saving devices?' Five hundred heads shake. 'Do you have more time than she did?' – the audience falls about laughing!

The other day I heard of a man knocking on doors trying to sell Ewbank carpet sweepers. His line was, 'It'll save you getting the hoover out every day.' One weary housewife replied, 'When I bought the hoover, the man said it would save me getting the Ewbank out every day.'

We are sinking under the weight of time-saving devices – and yet we seem to have less and less time. Nobody has enough time, yet everybody has all the time there is available. It is the one thing that the poorest beggar and the managing director of the largest company in the world have the same amount of. Surveys show that in industrialised countries, it is the thing that people want more of – twenty-five per cent want more money, but forty-seven per cent crave more . . . time.[1]

And it seems that families also crave this elusive commodity. Wives crave it from their husbands, husbands from wives, children from parents. And the inability to give that time is destroying homes. Life is so very busy.

We saw a wonderful illustration on a greetings card the other day. It was of a mum driving one of those space wagons with a dozen seats in it. She was obviously just at the end of some mammoth taxi job and had deposited her children at a multitude of different activities. She looked weary, hassled and puzzled. The reason she was puzzled was that she was gazing at a small boy who sat alone in the otherwise empty vehicle and she was saying, 'If Peter's at Cubs, and Susan's at piano, Simon's at karate and Lucy's at ballet – who on earth are you?'

That kind of living has been described as the 'rat race'. I am a lawyer, and somebody told me that in America scientists now use lawyers instead of rats for experiments. Apparently, that's for three reasons. Firstly, there are more lawyers than rats. Secondly, surveys have shown that the public are more attached to the rats. But thirdly, they have found that the lawyers are prepared to do things that the rats refuse to do! I can remember some years ago saying to Dianne, 'You know, darling, I would love to get out of the rat race.' Do you know what I have discovered? At heart, I'm a rat. I love the hurly and the burly – the busyness of it all. If I'm on my way to an appointment and find I'm going to be twenty minutes early, I'm tempted to fit in another meeting and a phone call on the way. But I have also learnt that if you live like that in the family, love dies, because love is based on relationships . . . and relationships need time.

The real cost of busyness

Let me take you to a meal table. It's about six in the evening. A man has been at work all day. His wife, too, may have just got in from work, or been at home with the children and would love to talk to him, but has long since given up at that hour of the day. But two small children are determined to try! One says, 'Dad, I came second in spelling today, and Peter pulled my hair again.' Not to be outdone, a five-year-old chips in, 'My teacher was nasty to me again, and Mark's goldfish has had babies.' But the man is silent. He grunts over the top of the newspaper. The truth is, this is a busy man. He's had a busy day, and he has an even busier evening in front of him – his mind is totally preoccupied. Nothing his family can say or do seems capable of bringing him out of this comatose state. But then the telephone rings and a small voice says, 'Dad, it's for you.' And suddenly that man comes alive and he's dispensing his ideas, his strategies, his opinions . . . and a little boy and a little girl are watching him. They're not kicking and screaming or banging on the table – it would be better if they were – but the message they are getting loud and clear is, 'This matters to him – this brings him alive.'

'Hey dad, will you play on the computer with us tonight?' 'Not tonight, son,' he says, 'I've got to go to a meeting. Tomorrow – we'll do it tomorrow.' The sad thing is that the child doesn't argue. He accepts it with an inevitability that has the seeds of tragedy in it.

Now we fast forward. It's 11.45 p.m. and he's still not in. His wife lies in bed. He's not with another woman, and he's not getting drunk. But he's not with her either. In fact, they haven't had an in-depth conversation for months. The bitterness rises in her against her will.

This man is highly thought of by others. He is just the kind of person you would want to be involved with if you needed to make things happen. He spends much of his life helping others. He's a good man. But in reality he's lost his wife, and his children are orphans.

Forgive me if that seems too emotional, but I cannot write about that man dispassionately, for I meet him so often in the letters that we receive, and I have made so many of those mistakes myself.

I would say that fifty per cent of the letters we receive raise the issue of spouses who are too busy to listen, let alone talk. Typical would be this:

My husband is a faithful husband and father, but he is so busy. As well as having a full-time secular job, he is on many committees and so involved in our local church. The kids and I don't see much of him. I'm getting bitter, but I feel I can't tell anybody else how I feel. I just don't want him to think I don't support him. The other wives seem to cope OK. Is it me? At home he doesn't talk much . . .

I am sure that such a man is popular with others. I am convinced that others look at him with admiration, even feeling a little intimidated by his ability to be involved in so much. What they, and sadly he, have no idea of is the price that is being paid for that life of furious activity. This man may bless the whole world, but his own family will feel isolated from him.

I can remember, some years ago, a friend saying to me, 'Rob, you seem to be so very busy. Have you heard the old Eastern proverb, "If you do this, you can't do that"?'

Time is limited. You can't buy it, mortgage it, or rent it. You can't even save it. We talk of 'saving time', but that's impossible, because as soon as we save it, we spend it, and every spending choice we make precludes another.

But I knew that wasn't true, because I'd been to the circus and I'd seen him – the spinning-plate man. I was nine years old when my dad took me. I watched wide-eyed as he went through his act. First, he took just one plate, put it on a pole, spun it, and – hey presto! – it stayed up. I would have clapped just for that, but he had greater ideas. He had fifty plates, and he put them all on poles and got them all spinning. So I knew it was possible to keep all the plates spinning at once. What I didn't know, as a small boy of nine, was that it was only possible for three minutes. If, at the end of his show, we'd yelled, 'Encore, do it again, do it again!', he would have rushed from plate to plate as he tried to do what we wanted. But soon the plates would have begun to fall and he would have stumbled as he tried so hard to keep them all going . . . forever. And finally, if we had yelled, 'Do it again! Do it again!', enough times, he would have lain broken among the shattered plates. You can run several agendas in life, but you cannot run them all at a hundred per cent without somebody paying a price. And so often, we who are living at the centre of the hurricane are the last to pay the price. Those around us whom we love pay the real cost.

The great illusion

We have so many excuses. The main one is that we convince ourselves a slower day is coming. We say to ourselves, 'When the house is decorated, when I get my promotion, when I've passed those exams – then I'll have more time.' Every time we have to say to a small child, 'Not now, darling – mummy's busy,' we tell ourselves it's OK because that slower day is getting nearer. It's as well that we realise, here and now, that the slower day is an illusion – it never comes.

We once bought a house in the winter. After being in it a short time, we noticed that the garden was a continual mud bath. The water would not drain away. We looked forward to the summer days when it would have a chance to dry out and we could let the children play outside without their coming in looking as if they'd had a session with the SAS. But that day never did come. Oh, the long hot summer days came, but that old lawn was just as wet. And then we discovered it – a spring that lay just underneath the surface.

Our 'slower days' are a little like that. They never come, because for most of us the problem is not from outward circumstances, but is a busyness created from *within*.

We have seen that busyness manufactured in the homes of fast-track executives and in the lives of those who at the moment are unemployed. Whatever our situation, we all have the potential to fill our time. That's why we need to *make time* for the things that we believe are important – and we need to make it now.

In our home, we used to have a hamster. In the inimitable way that children have of fitting names to personalities, they christened him 'Spinner'. That creature would sleep all day, and then at seven in the evening, it would climb on the wheel. It would pound that wheel hour after hour, with short breaks for food and water, and then get back on the wheel. Some days, I would stand in front of the cage and just watch him. I would want to say, 'Spinner, what would it take to get you off the wheel? What would it take?' I could imagine that little animal saying, 'It's impossible: I'm a hamster – life is meant to be like this. I was born to pound the wheel!'

I can remember a couple coming to me once and saying, 'Rob, what you have said about time pressure is so true. We would love to have more time for each other and for our two children, but we have a business and we simply can't stop.' But one day they *will* stop – the business will not consume them for ever as it does now. The big question is: when they do stop, will it be too late?

It must have been such a thought that inspired Robert Herrick to write:

Gather ye rose buds while ye may,
Old Time is still a-flying:

And that same flower that smiles to-day,
To-morrow will be dying.[2]

Breaking the mould

Is it possible to do anything about the slavery to time pressure which is destroying so many of our homes? The short answer is 'yes' – but long before techniques and time-management courses, we need a deep motivation that craves to change.

One of the most frequent questions that I am asked after a family seminar is, 'You seem to have a busy schedule – what about time with your own family?' My answer is to relate how, years ago, I made serious mistakes in this whole area. I was involved in my normal daily work, was a leader in a local church, was active in university speaking, was on numerous committees and was trying to be involved in a dozen other agendas. My family was paying the price of my over-busy lifestyle.

The realisation of several things brought about change in my life. First, it struck me that although it is true that we must put God before our families, I had misunderstood what that means. It does not mean that we are meant to take on so much activity that we neglect those for whom God has given us primary responsibility. The answer to the question, 'Which comes first, your family or the church?' is: 'My family is part of the church.' In any event, the credibility of any Christian service is affected if we do it at the expense of those we love.

Next, I realised that one of the lessons I had to learn was when it was legitimate to say no. Most of us love to say yes. We want to feel wanted, and we want others to approve of us. The problem is that when we agree to do everything that we are asked, it makes it difficult for us to find our real priorities. Jesus was faced with that. There were many who wanted him to fulfil their particular agenda, but he had such a clear view of what he was meant to be doing. This allowed him, at times, to use that liberating word, 'No.' 'Will you be our king?' – 'No.' 'Will you come back to the village we have just left, everybody is looking for you?' – 'No, we're going on to the next town.' Somebody said that he achieved all that he did in three years because he did exactly what his Father told him to do. We cannot please everybody, and unless we know when it is right to say no, there is no hope that we will fulfil our real priorities, including finding a good quality of family life.

The Bible says, 'Try to have a sane estimate of your capabilities.'[3] For me, the outworking of that lesson is a long, hard battle. I love to say yes when asked to help, but I have learnt that if I am to do the tasks to which God has called me, including being a husband to Dianne and fulfilling my God-given responsibility to two young lives, I cannot please everybody.

Do I now get over-committed? Do we have moments in our family when time pressure builds until we all want to yell and scream? Yes, all those things still happen, but they happen much less frequently now, and we recognise more easily when we've got it wrong, and resolve to do better next time.

The third ingredient which caused me to change was the realisation that my children were growing up so fast and the door of childhood was closing so very quickly. Now, when we have blown it and the diary is crammed full of engagements, it makes me angry that I have been so foolish and I almost grieve for the price that I will pay in not being with them. You see, I know that those evenings of helping with the homework, or playing a board game, or perhaps listening to a teenager's traumas in the boyfriend arena – mundane though they may seem – can never be repeated. I can honestly say that, if I had to choose, I would rather be with my family than anybody else on the face of the earth.

But if we are to change, we need more than motivation;

we need some practical help. Let me share with you some lessons that Dianne and I have learnt down the years.

'Being there' – for each other

We all understand that good relationships need verbal communication, but that's not the whole story. Just 'being together' is part of building a strong marriage and family. It doesn't even have to be in shared interests so that you are both alternately exclaiming, 'Oh, my clay pot is coming on wonderfully – how's yours doing?' It may be simply sitting in the same room, each involved in different things; it could be buying things for the house, or going to school concerts *together*.

If it's true for our partners, it's also true for our children. Parents do not need the pressure that, during every waking moment, they must be 'doing' things with their children. If we live like that, we'll drive ourselves and the children bananas. The great mystery is that, so often, they don't want us to 'do' anything with them. They just want us to be there when they are doing things. We would be mistaken if we believed this ended when they reach the teenage years. Many of us crave the security of just the *presence* of another person.

Planned time

A management consultant once advised a man whose wife was complaining that she never saw him to plan his spouse into his business diary as another engagement. I hope his wife never found the diary! Nevertheless, although that seems a little clinical, the truth is that if we are consistently going to have time together – husbands and wives, parents and children – we are going to need to plan it.

The best way for that to happen is if it's regular time. It may be that every Tuesday evening a couple try to spend time together. This doesn't have to have a price tag attached to it. It may just be a walk together, or an hour spent with the phone off the hook and the door barred! If you have older children, it's harder to get that time alone, but you still need it. The sad fact is, many couples don't have an evening like this once a month, let alone once a week.

Protected time

We need to defend these times with our lives! As soon as we agree them, great battalions will line up to make sure that we won't have that time together. The greatest incentive to winning the war is to understand the price of losing it. It is my belief that there are couples married for twenty-five years who, in all that time, have not had twenty-five minutes where they have sat in a quiet room and listened to each other without interruption. 'Darling, tell me your fears, tell me your dreams, tell me anything about me that drives you crazy.' Not twenty-five minutes in twenty-five years – and it tears the heart out of love.

'If you do this, you can't do that' – spending our time wisely

The biggest incentive for doing this is to have a sense of priority – to grasp the things that are really important in our lives. It's so easy for those we love to get squeezed out, and sometimes, because they love us and don't want to put pressure on us, they are the last to complain. But without time with each other it's hard for love to grow. This is how one wife put it:

> My husband is a successful company person. He has all the trappings – a company car, good suits, Gold Card, leather briefcase, and 'Filofax'. But he spends so little time with us. He is too busy ever to take an interest in

the things that the children do during the week – even if there is something on at school. Why does he not want to be home with us? My daughter said that she suspects people think she has no father – no one knows him.

We say to ourselves, 'If only I had more time,' but that is the one thing we will never have more of . . .

And so all men run after time, Lord.
They pass through life running – hurried, jostled, over-
    burdened, frantic, and they never get there. They
    haven't time.
In spite of all their efforts they're still short of time, of a
    great deal of time.
Lord, you must have made a mistake in your calculations.
There is a big mistake somewhere.
The hours are too short,
The days are too short,
Our lives are too short.

You who are beyond time, Lord, you smile to see us
    fighting it.
And you know what you are doing.
You make no mistakes in your distribution of time to
    men.
You give each one time to do what you want him to do.

But we must not lose time
                waste time,
                kill time,
For time is a gift that you give us,
But a perishable gift,
A gift that does not keep.

Lord, I have time,
I have plenty of time,
All the time that you give me,
The years of my life,

The days of my years,
The hours of my days,
They are all mine.
Mine to fill, quietly, calmly,
But to fill completely, up to the brim,
To offer them to you, that of their insipid water
You may make a rich wine such as you made once in Cana
of Galilee.

I am not asking you tonight, Lord, for time to do this and
then that,
But your grace to do conscientiously, in the time that you
give me, what you want me to do.[4]

Many of the letters we get about time pressure in the
family are from wives who complain that their husbands
cannot or will not make the time to fulfil the role of father
to their children. This is such a crucial issue it deserves
consideration on its own. We'll look at it next.

4

A Word to Fathers

A husband once arranged to play golf with a few friends. When his colleagues got to the course, they noticed that he had four caddies with him. One of them remarked, 'That's a bit over the top, isn't it?' 'Oh,' the man replied vaguely, 'it's the wife's idea. She wants me to see more of the children.'

A national newspaper picked up the same theme and ran a feature entitled 'Where are the fathers?' It highlighted the fact that these days eighty per cent of dads do not pace the floor of the maternity ward's waiting-area; instead,they are in the labour room. They stand right next to their wives and have the privilege of actually witnessing this incredible miracle, even if some of them do feel in need of a shot of gas and air! The problem, says the article, is that the minute they leave the hospital, many of them lose any interest in sharing the task of parenthood.

These men do not leave the home; they do their best to provide for their families. These children are well fed, but they are starved of their father's *time*.

The survey quoted in the article suggested that the average time that fathers spend talking to their children is three minutes a day.

These dads are constantly saying, 'When I've finished the decorating,' or, 'When I get promotion, then we'll have more time.' The problem comes because they are not driven by those outward circumstances, but from within – and that leisurely period never does come. Before they know it, their children have grown up. Without that time input, it is so hard for relationships to grow.

As we try to help teenagers in the sexual arena, we are convinced that many girls are adopting promiscuous lifestyles not because they want sex, but because they are in pursuit of the love and affection of their fathers. A social worker who has worked for many years with teenagers who were categorised as 'difficult' said to me, 'Many of them are craving affection – they are desperate to be loved.'

The closing door of childhood

There is hardly a parent on the face of the earth who would not say, 'I want to spend more time with my children.' And yet the desire to do so seems to be not enough, so strong are the pressures that fight against it being fulfilled.

A father said to us recently, 'I have to work such long hours just to give the children what they need.' The danger is that we are constantly redefining what 'need' is. Most children would willingly settle for less 'things' and more time. We are seeing a generation of children, many of whom live as though 'fatherless'. As the pace of life gets ever faster and the situation worsens, society will begin to count the cost.

'Dad, can we play now? Dad, will you teach me to ride the bike? Can you help me with this for a moment? Dad, can we go out now, please?' 'Later, son, later . . . we'll do it later.' We say to ourselves, 'If only they'd just give me a little peace – if only they'd stop asking.' The problem is that one day our wish is fulfilled; but when it is, it so often coincides with a period in our lives when we want to spend time with them, but they have learnt to live without us. There comes a time when they stop asking. The actor Robin Williams put it like this, 'I wanted my father to spend time with me when I was young, but he wouldn't. When I was fifteen, he suddenly wanted to take me fishing, but by then it was too late.'

When he was young, Lloyd used to come into the bathroom in the morning and say, 'Dad, will you tell me a story while you're shaving?' Now, I am not on top form early in the morning. The last thing on earth I wanted to do was to have to make up some dramatic tale as I was rushing for work and, in any event, my head would have been buzzing with a hundred issues that I had to face that day.

But I remember the morning when it hit me that although I was involved in many exciting ventures, including the work of CARE for the Family, they will probably all be around in ten years, with or without me. But the days when that little boy would come up the stairs and say, 'Dad, can we have that story today?' were limited. There was a day already fixed when he wouldn't come. We had those stories together for so many years, but Lloyd doesn't make that request now. You may ask me, 'When did he stop?' The answer is, I don't know. It just faded out. If I had known, then I would have made more of that last morning.

It doesn't do to get too emotional about it. It's OK to skip pages some nights when we're reading them stories. The trouble is children are too clever. 'Silly mummy,' she says, 'you've missed forty-nine pages!' I used to be able to get a frog into a prince and back again – with nothing in between! No, we shouldn't get too emotional; but at the same time, we had better realise how fast the door of childhood closes.

That came home to me so forcibly one evening. Katie was twelve, and I went to her bedroom. Just before I went in, I knocked on her door. And I thought, 'Rob, why did you knock on Katie's door?' I'd never used to knock before going in. I know why. I knocked because something in my heart said to me, 'Rob, there's a young woman in your home now.' The previous evening, I had been watching television when that young woman had walked into my living room. It was as if for the first time I had noticed that, in truth, the child was gone. She didn't give me any notice – she just walked right in. I look forward to the future years with Katie, but no power on earth can open that door of childhood again.

In another survey of fathers,[1] the men were asked, 'How long do you think you spend each day in conversation with your toddlers?' Most men guessed at twenty minutes a day. To test this, the researchers put microphones on the fathers and their children to measure accurately the amount of parental interaction. Those busy men spent an average of thirty-seven seconds a day with their children, split into three encounters of between ten and fifteen seconds each. At the same time, those toddlers were watching upwards of twenty hours of TV a week. That's where they were getting their education.

I remember speaking to five young men. I'd spent three hours advising them on a strategy to help build their business. When I finished, I said, 'Do you mind if I ask you something?' (Frankly, I was going to ask it whether they minded or not.) 'Are any of you married with children?' Yes, they all were. I said, 'My great fear for you is that in ten years you'll be even wealthier than you are now, but you will have lived those years as paupers.' One said, 'I know what you mean.' He went on, 'I like to be in the office at seven, my alarm goes off at five-thirty. The other day, by mistake, it went off at eight and I was stamping around the house angrily. My six-year-old boy said, "What are you doing home at this time of day, dad? Will you take me to school?" I held his hand, and we played games all the way to school.' He said, 'I thought to myself, why don't I do this every day?' And why not? And could it be possible? Perhaps even once a week?

The apostle Paul wrote some incredibly challenging words in regard to our use of time. In his letter to the Ephesian Christians he urges them to use it wisely. 'Make the best use of time – of every opportunity – because the days are evil.'[2] He had the choice of one of two words for time. He could have chosen *chronos*, which means an era or an age of time. But he used the word *kairos*. That word means a period of time that will never be repeated. All our years with our children are *kairos* years. They can never be repeated. God has given them to us, they are our responsibility. They're not primarily the responsibility of the youth-group leader, or even the education system. They are our responsibility. And the door of childhood closes so quickly, and so finally.

None of us know how our children will turn out. We don't know what lies down the road for them, or what forces will come up against them. We have those precious childhood years to put into their lives strengths and beliefs and a foundation that will help them when we're not there. All of that takes time.

A cry came from the bedroom: 'Mummy, I'm scared!' 'I can't come right now,' yelled back a harassed mum. 'Then send dad!' 'He can't come either – he's busy – remember that God is with you.' There was silence for a moment, and then, 'Get up here! I need somebody with *skin* on!'

Quantity vs quality

The sobering fact is that as we give our children the dignity of time, we show them how God *the* Father thinks about them. It's hard these days to tell some teens that God is their Father because they have such a negative image of the earthly variety.

To give time is not always easy. Sometimes after seminars men come to me and say, 'Rob, I honestly believe what you have said with all my heart, but my job does take me away so much.' I tell them that I believe children can handle more easily a dad who's away a lot, but would rather be with them, than they can a man who's there all the time, but in his heart and in his spirit is always somewhere else. I'd say to those dads who have to be away: let your children know in a hundred and one ways you'd rather be with them, that they're your priority. And when you are with them, make them feel special, make them feel at that moment they have your one hundred per cent attention. And they'll say to their friends, 'My dad has to be away a lot, but he'd rather be with me.'

I hear some say, 'I can't give my children quantity time because we are so busy, so I give them quality time.' It's probably not enough. Most children need lots of time, and the chances of your child wanting to share his heart with you in the particular time slot allocated are slim. Some of the most precious times we have with our children are off the cuff – they're not planned. A teenage daughter may say to you as you pack the board game away, 'Dad, Simon asked me out today and I'm just not sure. What do you think?' You didn't have a slot in your diary to talk about a young woman's romantic trauma; in fact, the quality time of conversation was only ten minutes, but it wouldn't have happened if you hadn't ploughed your way around that Monopoly board for the best part of two hours. That may be why one experienced parent put it like this: 'When it comes to our children, there's no such thing as quantity time and quality time. There is only time that we spend with them and time that we don't.' The great cry that we hear from parents is, 'Kids today just won't listen to you.' It may just be that if we listen to them when they're five, six and seven, then they'll listen to us when they're fourteen, fifteen, sixteen.

I fully understand that it's almost impossible to consider these issues without feeling guilty (I feel guilty as I write this), but it's easy for that guilt to be misplaced. It's important to remember that none of us can guarantee how our children will turn out. There are no guarantees. I know that the book of Proverbs says, 'Train a child in the way he should go, and when he is old, he will not turn from it.'[3] But that's not a guarantee – it's a general principle. There are no guarantees. Adam and Eve had the perfect father and the perfect environment – but they went a way that God didn't want them to go. Some parents are bearing guilt for no good reason. My heart especially goes out to those whose children have flown the nest, and who may be saying to themselves, 'I have made so many mistakes, there's so much I'd love to change – but it's too late now.' It is almost *never* too late to begin to be the mother or father you were meant to be. That may mean ringing up a daughter tonight and saying, 'Darling, you're not living as we want you to live; in fact, you have turned your back on everything we hold dear. But we want you to know that we still love you. This home is always your home.' I remember saying that to a large audience, and when I turned around the chairman was in tears – for his daughter. It is almost never too late to be the mother or father that you were meant to be.

'He learnt to walk while I was away'

What a task parenting is. It has been said, 'There is no pain like parental pain.' On a more lighthearted note, I heard of a man who said, 'When I married, I had four theories of child-rearing and no children. Now I have four children and no theories!' We just don't know how they are going to turn out, and for that very reason, anybody who makes any negative comment about anybody else's children until their own are in their nineties is crazy.

But parenting is a high calling. We are almost standing in the shoes of God and creating. The sobering thing is how fast the opportunities of parenting pass. I know of no clearer explanation of that than Harry Chapin's song, 'Cat's in the Cradle':

My child arrived just the other day,
    he came to the world in the usual way –
    But there were planes to catch and bills to pay
    he learned to walk while I was away
        and he was talkin fore I knew it and as he grew he'd say,

I'm gonna be like you, Dad
you know I'm gonna be like you.

and the cat's in the cradle and the silver spoon
Little boy blue and the man in the moon
when you comin' home, Dad

I don't know when
but we'll get together then –
you know we'll have a good time then

My son turned 10 just the other day
he said, Thanks for the ball, Dad, com'on let's play
Can you teach me to throw?
I said not today, I got a lot to do
He said That's okay
and he walked away but his smile never dimmed
it said I'm gonna be like him, yeah
you know I'm gonna be like him

and the cat's in the cradle and the silver spoon
Little boy blue and the man in the moon
when you comin' home, Dad

I don't know when
but we'll get together then –
you know we'll have a good time then

Well he came home from college just the other day
so much like a man I just had to say
Son, I'm proud of you, can you sit for awhile
He shook his head and said with a smile –
what I'd really like, Dad, is to borrow the car keys
see you later, can I have them please?

When you comin' home, Son?
    I don't know when
    but we'll get together then
  you know we'll have a good time then

I've long since retired, my son's moved away
  I called him up just the other day
  I said I'd like to see you if you don't mind
  He said, I'd love to, Dad – if I can find the time

You see my new job's a hassle and the kids have the flu,
  but it's sure nice talkin to you, Dad
  It's been nice talking to you

And as I hung up the phone, it occurred to me –
he'd grown up just like me; my boy was just like me

  and the cat's in the cradle and the silver spoon
  Like boy blue and the man in the moon
  when you comin' home, Son?
    I don't know when
    but we'll get together then, Dad,
  we're gonna have a good time then[4]

The will to change

Whatever changes we decide to make in these areas of our lives will involve a battle with that great enemy – time. Because if you do this, you can't do that. It may mean that if it's possible, we'll work fewer hours, maybe we'll play less sport or be involved in fewer activities outside the home (even church activities!). But somewhere we'll need to make time. And yet many of us are transfixed like rabbits in the headlights of a car; we see the most precious things we value slipping away from us, and we seem unable to move forward or back.

One father put it like this:

My family's grown up and all the kids are gone. But if I could do it over again, this is what I'd do:
- I would love my wife more in front of my children.
- I would laugh more with my children – at our mistakes and our joys.
- I would listen more, even to the smallest child.
- I would be more honest about my own weaknesses, never pretending perfection.
- I would pray differently for my family – instead of focusing on their shortcomings, I'd focus on mine.
- I would do more things together with my children.
- I would encourage them more and bestow more praise.
- I would pay more attention to little things, like deeds and words of thoughtfulness.
- I would share God more intimately with my family. Every ordinary thing that happened in every ordinary way I would use to direct them to God.[5]

One of the most moving letters I have ever received was from a seventeen-year-old girl whose father had died when she was five:

Mum has coped amazingly well and I'm so very proud of her. Occasionally, though, it does make me sad to think what I'm missing out on, especially when I hear other fathers talk about those special moments. However, I've got God as my father, and if daddy were alive, he would be an amazing father. What really upsets me are those fathers who have *chosen not to be with their children*.

I was thrilled to read of this child's relationship with her mum. Somebody should say it loud and clear that so many lone parents are doing a fantastic job. They need all the support we can give them. But two things are evident. Contrary to what some would have us believe, the vast majority of those mums would prefer that their children had a father's influence as well. The double tragedy is when, because of over-busy lifestyles or simply misplaced priorities, children live under the same roof as both parents but are starved of the love of one of them.

How do we begin to change? Any progress will involve at least two elements – an act of the will and a little planning. It may be special evenings during which the phone is unplugged, regular 'dates' with a teenage daughter, or perhaps simply making that model together. It may not seem a great deal, but it will mean so much to these children, because it gives them the thing that we all crave . . . a sense of dignity – that we matter.

When God wanted to convey to us the depth of his care and the quality of his relationship with us, time and time again it was the same word that he chose – 'Father'. It's a high calling.

A 'PS'

This is just a thank-you for all the women who have read this chapter. I'm sure it won't be a surprise to you to know that the vast majority of those who have read it *will be women*. It's hard to get men to read books on family life, but all that I have shared about the vital role of fathers is, of course, true for mothers. They too face the fact that the childhood years pass so very quickly. All of that was brought home to me so strongly by a poem sent to me by a mum:

She's gone.
The child I once knew –
and in her place –
a woman
vulnerable –
lacking polish
needing assurance perhaps
but nevertheless
a woman.
The pain of her birth into womanhood
was every bit as great as the pain of her birth
the more so perhaps because of its
suddenness
then there were months of waiting
of preparation
now in a day –
separation
She's gone.

She's gone
And I must let her go –
time now for painful rebuilding
where innocence – now knowledge
where wondering – now certainty
where hesitancy – now assurance
where once childlike trust
now I must accept a woman's vulnerability

Viewpoints considered – decisions made
– without me
ideas formulated carefully
girlhood pushed back
– womanhood embraced
as she steps from my arms into his.

But I will wait
Not in desperation – but patiently
for she may need me yet
as man needs man
and woman needs another woman –
and we will walk together she and I
side by side.
For my child is gone
and in her place –
a woman.[6]

If we want to build relationships we have to win the battle with time, but it's not the only issue. Even when we do make time it can be so hard to communicate – to actually be able to let another person know how we feel and to appreciate what they are experiencing. For that most of us need a little practical help . . .

5

Hey – Look Who's Talking!

The power of communication is awesome, the difficulties of non-communication great, but the penalties of hasty communication are frightening, as the following story illustrates.

I have worked in offices for over twenty years, and honestly thought that I had seen most of the really hysterical typing errors that were possible, but the other day, I came across a story that made previous mistakes pale into insignificance.

A businesswoman had been favoured with an interview by an elderly managing director who was both very influential and very hard to please. She was hoping that he would give her company a considerable amount of work, so she prepared meticulously. Eventually the great day came, and to her delight it seemed to go reasonably well; in fact, as she left he shouted, 'Looking forward to doing business with you.'

Feeling elated, she rushed back to her office, determined to get a letter straight off to him, saying how grateful she was that he had given her his time. Unfortunately, when she got there her secretary had left, but she was no mean typist herself and quickly had the letter in the post.

Not only did the hoped-for work not come, but when she happened to bump into the great man a few months later, he was decidedly frosty. With a sinking feeling in the pit of her stomach, she went to her filing cabinet and re-read the letter she had sent: 'Thank you for spending time with me *toady* . . . I look forward to seeing you *son*!'

We smile at her difficulty, but the truth is that many of us find it hard to communicate well – even with those we love. Lack of communication is the number one difficulty referred to in the letters we receive at CARE for the Family. A woman writes of a man who, in the factory canteen, is the life and soul of the place. Any lunch-time will find him surrounded by his friends as he cracks jokes or tells them his latest opinion on some issue of the workplace. But in the evening he's so different. One wife put it like this, 'It's as if he's had a conversation by-pass operation on the way home from work!' His wife and children struggle to learn what this man, who is so central to all their lives, thinks, feels – even wants.

A husband writes of his wife, who runs a small business. She spends her life communicating – by letter, by telephone, by fax – but it's almost as if she uses all her words before she sees her family. She is so good at communicating information – but not feelings – it's as if there's nothing to say.

Church leaders are often great communicators, they spend their lives talking and listening to others, but they so often tell me that they find it hard to share their hearts at home, to listen to those near to them. Some will say they find it difficult to pray. In short, communication with those they really care about has all but died. One leader's wife summed it up like this: 'It is agony seeing my husband come to life in the pulpit, when we seem to have lost something so precious in our own communication.'

I identify with this so strongly. I remember returning home after speaking at a marriage seminar. I had just driven two hundred miles, and it was the early hours of the morning. So as not to disturb Dianne, I slipped into the guest bedroom; there was a note on the pillow: 'Darling,

I love you, but we haven't talked much together recently and I'm missing it.' I had just spent an evening with five hundred people, helping them communicate in their own marriages, and here was my own wife saying, 'Rob, let's not forget what we preach – let's go on working at it.'

There are many reasons why we find it so hard to communicate. One we have already mentioned – the sheer pressure of life today. Someone has put it like this, 'Too pooped to pop!' Another reason why it's so hard is that in this busy world many of us have lost the ability to communicate with *ourselves* – and that makes it hard to talk in depth with others. We find it difficult to sit alone in a room without wanting noise in some form – perhaps television; we find it hard to drive without the radio on, and certainly we can't remember the last time we went for a walk for no other purpose than to spend time alone. We have little to say – even to ourselves. Some years ago, a friend pointed this out to me. He said, 'Rob, you live such a busy life, you seem to have lost the art of communicating with yourself.' He suggested that I go for regular walks and do what he called 'Kicking the leaves'. It was a lovely image: to amble, not hurry to some particular destination, and just enjoy the sheer luxury of discovering a little of myself again. He told me that if I got a brilliant idea for work I shouldn't break my neck to find a telephone and get somebody involved in it: rather, I should put it on the back-burner for the moment. This was an exercise in learning to spend time with myself.

The reason so many of us find it hard to pray is that we have lost the knack of even communicating with our own heart, let alone with the God who made us.

If the first secret of communication in marriage is that we need to learn to talk to ourselves, the second is, of course, that we have to learn to talk to each other. And therein lies a challenge, because the minimum requirement for that to happen is that we spend time together. Some of those times will be short – moments snatched here and there – but if we are to really communicate, some will need to be planned. Let's look at those two situations.

How to change your marriage in less than ten minutes!

Leonard Zuin said, 'The two most important periods in a marriage relationship are the first four minutes in the morning and the last four at night.' I believe that there is much truth in that. The way we react to each other on waking, and the atmosphere that surrounds us as we go to sleep, are important. Somebody once asked the wife of a friend of mine, 'In the morning, do you wake up grumpy?' 'No,' she replied ' – he normally comes around himself!'

Whatever you make of Zuin's 'four-minute rule', there's no doubt that good communication can take place in relatively short periods of time – if we are prepared to *make time* to talk. We may be on a car journey together and, instead of reaching for the radio button, we'll at least wait to give conversation a chance.

The vast majority of these times will not be outstanding romantic moments; we could be changing a nappy, or doing the dishes, but don't look down on these times – they will form the largest part of our communication. The truth is that many marriages would be revolutionised by ten minutes of meaningful conversation a day.

Only one warning! Let's be sensitive to times when our partner is physically exhausted and actually needs resuscitation, not conversation! For most mums with small children, the period between four and six will not be the time when they are at their most relaxed. One mother summed it up like this: 'If ever I run away from home, I'll surely leave at 5.15!'

Long-term planning!

Although much of our communication will be fitted around other needs, we will all benefit from times which are more relaxed, when we can talk in depth. Those times will normally need a little planning. These are occasions when we're not absolutely shattered, the phone is off the hook, and when we say no to others so that we can begin again to build strong relationships with each other.

The first thing we have to acknowledge is that the second we agree to have that time together, it's as if the whole world conspires to make it impossible. We find that somebody has altered the date of the committee meeting and 'everyone else can make it on that night'. It's vital at this time to realise that this *is* a battle, and we are going to need commitment to win. We must have the courage to say 'I'm sorry, I can't make it then – I already have an appointment.' You may think that selfish, and say, 'But my husband and I could arrange another night.' You could, but you probably never will.

The challenge of the committee meeting is now beaten off, but there are a dozen other ambushes in place, every one of them bent on robbing us of that time to talk. We are beginning to understand how it must have been for Custer! Sometimes, of course, we don't fight those battles as hard as we might. It may be that the thought of an evening together when we actually have to begin the process of communication seems a bit daunting, and the committee meeting suddenly takes on the attraction of a weekend in Paris!

But finally the evening comes – and with it two further challenges that are much harder. The first is from the children – they demand our time. The way in which we deal with this will of course depend on their age, but the ground rules are best laid when they are very small. The basic principle is this: 'mum and dad love you so much, and time with you is more important to us than with anybody else on the face of the earth – with one exception: we

64

need time with each other. That will help our love grow strong and help us all to be the family God wants us to be.'

We are committed to encouraging parents to spend time with their children, but not at the expense of their own relationship. So often, when a husband and wife are going through a difficult time, one of them will compensate by giving excessive attention to the children – time, emotion, even 'adult' conversation. But we usually do the children no favours by doing this, and we lose the resolve to sort out the heart of the problem. That's why Louis M. Terman said, 'If a wife doesn't love her husband more than she loves her children, both the children and the marriage are in danger.'

The second challenge to our time together comes not from the children, but from the telephone. If we are going to have some quality time together, there must be some protection from that instrument. It is the rudest of all interrupters. The story goes that the British Ambassador in Washington went to see President Roosevelt, but Roosevelt kept taking telephone calls. Finally, the ambassador stalked out, rang Roosevelt and had an hour and a half uninterrupted on the telephone! You must decide how you fight this battle – it may mean investing in phones that unplug, or getting somebody else to answer it for you. It may mean that your special evening is held in a McDonalds or, if you have children and can't get a baby-sitter, sitting in the car in your own drive!

Wherever it is held, this needs to be viewed as a precious evening – and protected.

Learning to talk

Well, we've made it. We are actually sitting next to each other – alone! And the agenda is: conversation! Now here lies another little problem, and it's simply that when we've had a long period in our marriage without good communication, then to find it again is almost like learning to play the piano. It demands practice, and that may mean going through a pain barrier. One of the partners will say:

'Well, we're supposed to communicate – shall we turn the television off?'

'Just turn it down for now; what do you want to talk about? You go first.'

'No, you go first – it was you who wanted to do this.'

'OK, let's talk about your mother.'

'No, I don't want to talk about my mother. If you're going to be like that, why don't we talk about the way you ruined Christmas? I have never felt so humiliated in all my life!'

'You felt humiliated! You mean like I feel every time you make that stupid joke about my cooking?'

And so the conflict starts. In fact, every marriage has at least six bazookas that the partners bring out in times of conflict. They are very old and very boring. We would do well to lay them down, if only to find new ones! But even if that kind of conflict comes when we try to communicate, it's worth going through the pain barrier. The problem with some marriages is not that the partners row, it's that they don't row enough. Instead, they develop the creeping separateness which we looked at in an earlier chapter. The hurts are all internalised. They are not forgotten. In fact, they grow in secret.

Getting going in the conversation is something that most of us could use a little help with, and certainly Dianne and I find that to have a conversation 'starter' eases us into in-depth communication. The 'starter' is often not important in itself, and you soon wander to the things that are on both your hearts. You might find some of the following helpful. If you don't need any help, rip out this page and use it to light the candles!

- If you could do anything, go anywhere, be anyone, what would those choices be?
- Ask each other to name the things in your marriage that you appreciate most.
- If you could change three things about your marriage, what would they be?
- If you could change one thing about yourself, what would it be?
- If you could change one thing about your partner, what would it be?
- Discuss how much time you and your partner spend talking to each other in an average day: five minutes, between a quarter of an hour and an hour, between one and two hours, more than two hours? Are you satisfied with the amount of time? If not, what would you like to change it to?
- At what time of day do you find it easiest to talk? Under what circumstances do you find it easiest to talk: eating a meal, walking, working on something together, in the car?
- What do you wish that you could discuss more?
- Competing priorities can make it hard to spend time together. What priorities do each of you have for your life and your family?
- What does the Bible mean when it says, 'Love keeps no record of wrongs' and 'Love always protects, always trusts, always perseveres?'
- Busyness is a major problem in communication. What changes could you make in your home to make more time for each other?
- If somebody suddenly left you £500, what would you spend it on?

You may find that during those conversations the time flies by or drags at first; but, either way, if often helps to put a time limit on those occasions – so long as there's another one planned soon and things begun but not resolved can be carried on then.

There are many lessons that we'll learn along the way. It may be that at first there are long silences. As we get used to each other in this context, we'll feel less and less need to fill every moment with words.

Above all, be gentle with each other. If you know that your partner finds it hard to share their heart, be patient, and remember that if an argument develops, as it well might, winning is not normally anything like as important as it appears to be.

How to be a great communicator

I used to find it so difficult to talk easily on a one-to-one basis with anybody. I often speak to large audiences, but the prospect of coffee after church would fill me with dread. I'm still more comfortable with five hundred than five, but I have learnt some lessons. One of the great difficulties was that I felt I had nothing to say. I prided myself that small talk wasn't my thing, but I knew it was deeper than that: I was struggling in communication.

Then something happened that changed my life in that area. I still won't be the most exciting person to talk to in the party, but at least these days I don't hide in the bathroom. So what was this big revelation? Very simply – I began to observe somebody who was a great communicator. At every gathering, he would be mixing freely, irrespective of the status of the person to whom he was speaking. He was sought out by others who simply wanted to talk to him. As I watched, I longed to be able to do what he did, and then one day it hit me, I could, because what he did was *listen*. As I watched him, I noticed that he hardly said a word. He may have been a great communicator, but his secret was that he took an interest in the lives of others – he was a great listener!

Listening is vital to good communication – and it is so different to hearing. We have all heard a mother or father scream at a toddler, 'Listen to me when I talk to you!' She doesn't mean 'hear me'. In fact, anybody in the Western hemisphere can pick up the gist of the conversation! No, she is saying, 'I want you to *listen*.' When we hear, we understand what is being said; but when we listen, we *feel* it. Paul Tillich was right, 'The first duty of love is to listen.' To be a good listener is seventy five per cent of being a good communicator.

Partners so often complain that somebody outside the marriage listens to them better than their spouse. 'If only I could talk to you like I can talk to Mary,' she says. There are at least three reasons for this. The first is very basic. It's just that it's easier to take somebody for granted if you live with them for twenty-four hours a day, and we generally have to work harder to make those conversations stimulating.

The second is that because of work commitments, most of the times married couples have for communication are in the late evening, when they are both shattered.

Lastly, it's not so hard to have a meaningful conversation with somebody when the person we're talking to doesn't have an agenda that may be against us. They are just good friends, giving time to listen and sympathise, not a husband or wife who is thinking, 'When he said that, was he complaining about me?'

It *is* easier for friends, but most of us in marriage could do with a week's course on effective listening. We could be helped by the simplest things. A three-year-old was trying to get her father's attention, but he was busy reading a newspaper. As she tugged on his arm, she said, 'Daddy, daddy, listen to me read to you.' 'I am listening,' he said, continuing to scan the sports page. 'No, silly,' she said, 'you have to listen with your eyes as well!' It's true. The greatest dignity that we can pay to anybody who is talking to us is to have eye contact with them. There is nothing more infuriating than pouring out your heart to somebody, and suddenly realising that they're watching something that's going on behind you.

Good listening has so much to do, not only with the words that we speak, but with the signals that we give. It could be the tone of our voice. 'What did I say wrong?' she asks. He replies, 'It's not what you said, it's just that you've got that "know it all" tone in your voice again.'

It could be that our body language gives the signal that we're not really interested in what somebody is saying – arms folded defensively, eyes wandering around the room. The opposite is to give body language that says, 'I'm with you' – occasional touches, nods, smiles and eye contact. All these say, 'Keep going, I'm receiving you – there's life on this planet!' There's no doubt about it, great communicators are great listeners. The Bible sums it all up: 'Everyone should be quick to listen, slow to speak . . .'[1]

GOOD LISTENERS DON'T:
- Interrupt.
- Finish sentences for other people.
- Let anybody see them looking at the clock.
- Answer the phone if that gives the message that the phone call is more important than the conversation they're already having.

In short, good listeners try to give the kind of dignity to others that God gives us when we pray – a sense that nobody else in the whole world is praying right now, and the belief that *we matter*.

How to share your heart when you're lost for words

One of the greatest difficulties in communication is finding the right words for what we want to say. The phrase that really sums it up is, 'I'm lost for words.'

Carey and Shane found it difficult to articulate how they really felt, so one night Shane sat down and put some of his feelings in a letter:

Dearest Carey,
We seem to find it so hard to talk any more, and we always end up rowing. I am beginning to feel as if our love for each other is dying. I can't tell you how hurt I feel that you just won't talk about it any more. I think I understand why you feel like that, because I know that for most of our married life, it has been you pleading with me to sit down and talk things through. Neither of us is very good at it, but I just know that if we don't try, there's no hope for us. I am really sorry for the way I hurt you on Friday. It's just that sometimes when we row, you seem to be much better with words and I feel cornered.
Carey, I love you.

Sometimes a letter like that, which sets out simply some deep feelings, without being threatening, is more effective than spoken words in getting real communication going.

Another alternative is the use of 'word pictures'. These are an attempt to say how you feel by creating a word image for the other person to see. Many of the greatest communicators of all time have used them – Jesus especially. A word picture is a communication, spoken or written, that uses a story or object to reach both the emotions and the intellect of a person. In so doing, it causes the person to *experience* our words, not just hear or read them.[2]

Here's an example: Simon had begun an affair and walked out of Susan's life – left her with Sarah, aged five, and Daniel, just six months old. He would occasionally call to see the children, and she tried so hard to let him know how she felt, but they always ended up rowing. Then one day she wrote him a note. When he first opened it he braced himself for the usual tirade of criticism, but as he began to read he knew that this letter was different.

Dearest Simon, I understand that the last thing you want from us is any more interference in the new life that you have chosen. But we all love you so very much, and I wanted to try to explain how we feel about losing you.

Last night, I had a dream. It was a beautiful summer's day, and somebody offered to lend you a little boat to take us sailing. (Must have been prompted by bathing Daniel!) The children were so excited, and for a while we all just enjoyed the sheer adventure of it all. The sun was hot on our faces and the world seemed so very perfect. And then, suddenly, the weather changed. It became cold and dark, great flashes of lightning were tearing the sky in half, and the sea became very rough. The boat began lurching, and we fell from end to end. For a moment, I lost sight of you as you lurched towards the back of the boat. The children were crying, and I was so desperately afraid. I clutched Sarah to me and turned to hand Daniel to you, but you were gone.

At first I thought you had fallen overboard, but then I saw you. A large yacht was nearby. It was so grand it seemed to dwarf our boat, and you were on it with another woman. But that yacht wasn't in the storm; it seemed so secure and so very serene. You were putting a cardigan over her shoulders to keep off a gentle breeze. But Simon, we were dying. We called to you, but the big boat started its engines and moved slowly away.

And then, Simon, came the worst part. The children were hurt and I was hugging them to me. But then, as suddenly as it started, the storm stopped and the sea around our little boat became calm. We strained our eyes to see the yacht in the distance. And then we saw it, but the storm had hit it too, and much more fiercely even than it had caught us. And Simon, the great ship was sinking. We watched it die. We had all lost so very much.

When Simon got that note, it was as if he saw for the first time what his affair was doing to his family, and where it was all leading. It communicated to both his mind and his heart.

Communication is the heart of a relationship, and if we are to develop it in our marriage, it will almost certainly involve us in a battle with that great enemy, time. We may watch less television, perhaps be involved in less activity outside the home, or if possible work fewer hours. For most of us, this will not come easily; it will be an ongoing commitment. I met a man the other day who said to me, 'Rob, you talk a lot about men finding it hard to communicate, but in our marriage, it's my wife who won't talk in depth.' I asked, 'Has it always been like that?' His head went down and he said, 'No, she used to beg me to spend time with her, but I was so busy. And then suddenly, it changed. It was as if her love had died.'

When the children were small, I would kiss them goodnight and say, 'I'll be up in a moment to say prayers.' Those times weren't just prayer, but close times of sharing the events of the day, perhaps even the fears of tomorrow. But sometimes I would be in the middle of something and say to myself, 'I'll just finish this first.' And then, with the job finally done, I'd make my way upstairs. But sometimes I was too late. Although little eyes had fought to stay awake, they had lost the battle long ago. And I would stand there and wish with all my heart I had made a different choice.

That is so often how it is in communication between partners. The time comes when the busyness is gone, but it is now too late, and with all their hearts they wish they had made a different choice.

Good communication in marriage is not easy, and the helps in this chapter are not meant to make it seem easy, but to assist you a little in getting going. In truth, such communication is at times 'against the odds'. But if you have a will to share your heart with those you love, you will find a way that will be right for you . . . and it can happen to anybody. 'Hey – look who's talking!'

6

How to Fight a Good Fight

I once met a couple of whom it was rumoured that in many years of married life they had never had a row. It reminded me of a couple in their nineties. They had been married for over seventy years and everybody thought them blissfully happy. Then, out of the blue, they began divorce proceedings. Their friends were shattered and asked the obvious question, 'Why now, after all these years?' They practically replied together – it was obviously a strategy worked out long ago – 'We wanted to wait until the children were dead.'

The moral of the story is simple; when a couple tell you that they've never had a row, it's for one of three reasons: they're lying, their definition of a row is where one of the parties uses Challenger tanks, or, more likely, they don't talk to each other.

The truth is, wherever you have people, you have conflict. If we were to analyse the news bulletins, we would find that the largest proportion of them involve in some way the reporting of conflict. It may be conflict between unions and employers, or Government and opposition, it could be that we are ushered into the conflict of a foreign war zone, or asked to witness an inner-city riot.

People interacting with people produce conflict. For this reason, each of us has a list, long or short, of the 'difficult' people in our lives. It might be someone at work, or a neighbour. They seem so contentious, we dread meeting them. If it is someone from church, they so often preface disaster with, 'I've got something I want to say to you in love . . .' If anybody ever says that to you, get out of the way fast: something is about to drop on you from a great height. How we would love to be rid of the difficult people in our lives; if only they would get another job, find another church, life would be bliss! It's an illusion. It reminds me of the story of the railway company that decided because it was often the last carriage on the train that was involved in accidents, they would remove it!

The fascinating thing about difficult people is that they are always with us. It may be that one day you get the news that a difficult person is to leave your workplace. In fact, the person himself breaks the news to you one Monday morning. It seems they have the chance of promotion if they move to Alaska. You sympathise, mumble something about your loving white Christmases, and desperately try to stop yourself doing double cartwheels down the corridor. You begin to imagine how life is now going to be. And then you get a shock.

Almost as soon as they leave, somebody rises up to take their place; somebody who hitherto was only in the minor league of difficult people now rockets into the premier division. They are far more effective than the old ones ever were, and after a few months you find yourself wishing Albert back from snowier climes.

If we are to live life with a measure of peace and effectiveness, we had better get used to living with difficult people – because *we are somebody else's difficult person*. It is especially vital to grasp this with regard to those who are close to us.

Conflict is normally more intense and difficult to deal with when it is personal, and therefore the nearer it gets, the more it hurts. Normally conflict with the Government over the way it runs the country will hurt less than conflict with our boss over the way he runs the department, and that will often cause us less trauma than the way the vicar runs the church. The more emotional investment we have in something, the more conflict is something that we feel deeply.

And that's where marriage comes in. Higher even than conflict with parents (because we didn't choose them, and it's accepted that we can leave them) is discord with the man or woman that we have vowed to stay with until we die – the person that we sleep with, give our bodies to, and the mother or father of our children. And all that is true because, of all the people in whom we could have put our emotional investment, we chose them. We love them, or we believed that we would always love them – they matter to us.

The Bible is such a realistic book, and it never suggests that we will be able to live conflict-free lives; rather, it urges us to learn to deal with it. I'm sure many of you had the verse from Paul's letter to the Ephesians quoted to you in the early years of your married life. I remember on our wedding day standing there as it was read to Dianne and me, 'Do not let the sun go down while you are still angry.'[1] Someone has paraphrased it: 'Resolve the flack before you hit the sack.' It means simply that when conflict comes, we should try to resolve it quickly. The minister said to us, 'It means that you never go to bed not talking.'

I think it was good advice, but I have to tell you that Dianne is much worse at it than me. Sometimes we go to bed in stony silence, and Di will not give in! We both lie there huffing and puffing and pulling the sheets. After a while, I decide to go for reconciliation (if only to re-trieve a little of the duvet), and I'll touch Dianne's foot with my toe; Dianne immediately withdraws the whole leg. But, after a few hours of sighing and sheet-pulling, we normally manage at least to talk about it. I suppose it's progress that, although we didn't quite get it sorted before the 'sun went down', we began peace talks before it came up again!

Some couples go through twenty years and more of married life like that – huffing and puffing and pulling the sheets. 'I will not give way on that.' 'You will not beat me on this one.' 'I will not lose face again!' There is no machinery to resolve even small conflicts.

The strange thing about rows in a marriage is that, if we can learn to resolve them, then two days later we can't remember what the row was about. If we can't resolve conflict, then two days later we still can't remember what started it, but the bitterness goes on rolling down the years.

Some years ago a man said to me, 'I want to leave my wife.' I asked him what had led to this. I was expecting the reasons I have heard so many times – perhaps an affair, sexual difficulties, or some long-term conflict that had finally caused love to die. I will never forget his reply. He said, 'When I got home from night shift last night, she was out and had left for my main meal an unopened tin of pie filling.' I said, 'You're not serious – you can't be leaving your wife over that.' But he was adamant – that canned meal had ended his marriage. But it hadn't; it was rather that the incident built on a thousand others, all unresolved, that had just rolled down the years. Behind it was not even a meal; more a resentment that she was not home when he came in, and a growing frustration that they were growing apart, and she didn't care.

Those unresolved hurts are never forgotten; they are so often pushed to the back of the mind, where they lie for years and grow in secret. We see it so often as they are recalled years later, often in divorce proceedings. They were never dealt with.

In itself, the conflict is not normally the major issue. The real opportunities for both strengthening or breaking a marriage lie in how we deal with it. But to see it in those terms and use it positively, we first have to understand why conflict comes, and why it can be so very hard to deal with.

Great Expectations!

One of the main causes of conflict in marriage is that we become disappointed in our partner. We had expected so much more of them. We had never really believed we would ever have to love them *against the odds*. We live in an age where we are taught to have high expectations. Daniel Boorstin sums up that attitude like this:

> We expect anything and everything. We expect the contradictory and the impossible. We expect compact cars which are spacious, luxurious cars which are economical. We expect our two week holiday to be romantic, exotic, cheap and effortless. We expect a faraway atmosphere if we go to a nearby place. We expect to eat and stay slim, to be constantly on the move and ever more neighbourly. Never has a people expected so much more than the world could offer.[2]

Those high expectations are with us as we walk into married life together. It's interesting that in the early years of married life, couples are often very protective of each other. They quickly spring to each other's defence at the slightest hint of criticism. Someone has said, 'We think we've married a dream and we just don't want to wake up!' But as marriage progresses, we tend to develop a more realistic view of our partner. The problem is so often that we know what they're like now – and we don't like it. We look at our husband or wife and think, 'If only they could be like *her* husband, *his* wife.'

Let's listen in on a conversation; it's 11.15 p.m. and the participants are in bed:

'Why aren't you more like Bernard? Did you know that Bernard comes home every night and cooks the meal, washes up, hoovers through, cleans out the pets, and is building a jacuzzi in the loft?'

'No, dear, I didn't know that: but would you swap me for him?'

'Goodnight, Harry.'

We deserve to have some expectations, but they need to be realistic. You may have heard of the man who said to a friend 'I expect my wife to be the same in twenty years' time as she is now.'

'Walter, that's unreasonable,' came the reply. 'Yes,' said Walter wearily, 'that's what she is now.'

Those expectations could be to do with physical looks, with cooking or handyman abilities, they could have to do with priorities. A husband told me recently that what used to cause most conflict in their marriage was when they were invited out for a meal. His priority was to be there on time, hers was to look as good as possible. He said, 'Most of my anger was that I felt she was letting me down personally. It was agony until I realised that Susan was like that when I married her. I had subconsciously believed that I could change her so that she could be like me.' So much conflict is caused when we try to make our partner into somebody that we believe they ought to be. These are literally *clashes of personality*.

The truth is that we can rarely change our partner. But we can change ourselves, and because change is dynamic, that affects other people. If our partner is constantly bringing us down in public, we won't normally stop that by playing the same game – that will fuel it. But we may affect it by changing how we react to it.

Carol had suffered for many years with Tom making jokes about her weight in public. In the early years of her marriage she had borne that quietly, but with tremendous hurt. As the marriage went on she had begun to give as good as she got, and would reply with a withering comment about his intellectual ability. They had become a regular side-show at parties, and although some of their less discerning friends were enjoying the prospect of a night out with Tom and Carol, the continual barrage was affecting their relationship. Carol couldn't change Tom's behaviour, so she decided to change hers. One evening, she sat down and wrote him a letter:

Darling, I am writing because I feel I can better express in a letter how I feel about a situation that I am really scared will eventually break our marriage. Over the years I have come to hate the way that you treat me when we're with others, and I have foolishly tried to give back as good as I've got. Tom, I love you too much to see us going on tearing each other apart in public and I'm going to stop doing it. In future, when it happens, I am simply going to leave wherever we are. I know that will be embarrassing for both of us, but it's better than the slanging match that we're putting on at the moment. Let's both try.

Tom brought Carol down just *one more time*. He will never forget her getting up without a word and leaving the table at the home of one of their friends. He had never believed she'd do it, and he was so angry. In fact, when he got home that night they had one of the biggest rows of their married life. He screamed, 'You humiliated me!' and she replied, 'Tom, I didn't do it for that. I have just decided that although it seems that I can't change what you say about me in public, at least I don't have to listen to it.' You can have a meal with Tom and Carol now and they're still great company – but not at each other's expense.

Unseen baggage!

The handling of conflict would be so much easier if we started marriage with a clean slate of experiences, memories, and patterns of behaviour – but we don't. We come to it cluttered, staggering under the weight of past experiences, both good and bad. Some of those affect how we act in certain situations. We may think that we are one of the most flexible people on the face of the earth, but the pull of the past is strong.

You may have heard of the little girl who asked her mother, 'Mum, why do you always cut the ends off the joint before you put it in the oven?' 'Strange you should say that,' came the reply. 'Do you know, I don't really know; my mother used to do it. I imagine it must have something to do with letting the juices run. We'll ask Gran next time we see her.' Within a couple of days, the mystery had deepened. 'Well,' Gran had said, 'I'm not sure; my mother always did it. Let's ask her why.' Three generations of children piled into the car to visit Great Grandma and stood hushed, waiting for the answer. 'Great Grandma, why *did* you cut the ends off the meat? What wonderful culinary secret is contained in that?' Great Grandma chuckled. 'Well, my dears,' she said, 'I had such a small oven!'

How our past experiences affect us, and how tenaciously we hold on to them. And it's not just lessons from the kitchen that remain with us, but those from every room in a thousand different circumstances, and they cause us not just to *act* in a certain way, but to *react*.

Let's be a fly on the wall as a young couple return home two weeks after the wedding . . .

They have just got back from their honeymoon. The confetti is hardly out of their hair, and the memory of listening to all those cards being read is still alive in their brains. They wander around their new flat and into the spare room and there they are – the presents that loving friends and family have given. It is quite a selection: seven toasters, sixteen kitchen racks (which, when assembled, hold implements that nobody knows how to use), and tea towels – lots of them!

Just behind the gifts, and looking worn alongside their younger rivals, are two piles of personal belongings. They are heaped like mountains – the clutter of two lives. She had lived in her own flat for three years, and possessed a wide selection of life's necessities, including a bread bin, a food mixer (egg whisk missing), and a sink plunger. He, on the other hand, had come straight to the marriage from his parents' home, and his belongings seem to evidence a certain reluctance to sever old ties completely (is that really a teddy bear?). So there they are – the old and the new, all that this wide-eyed couple have to bring into their new life together. But wait. Where did those boxes come from, sitting, almost hidden, in the dusty corner of the room? The boxes are old, very old. The wood on each is worn with age, scarred from use, the brass of the handles dull with neglect and, on both, labels dated with the very years that this man and woman were born.

Who packed those boxes so tightly that they could scarcely be lifted? And, having packed them, who brought them, and what do they contain?

This man and this woman, now husband and wife, will find the answers. For *they* packed the boxes, packed them over twenty-five years – piece by piece, each with an entire life's history of emotions and experiences. Oh, they did not intend to bring those old things to this new house. But these boxes would not be left behind and, unknowingly, the newlyweds dragged them, bumped them over the threshold. And in their new life together, the contents – painful events, emotional scars, quiet expectations and well-used patterns of behaviour – will eventually be unpacked . . .

The boxes were opened on Tuesday night at seven o'clock. He got in late from work and the table was already laid.

They chatted as she served the meal. What he said next was not vicious or vindictive, nor even premeditated. He said, 'I think I'll have mine in the other room on a tray – there's a match on the television.'

The lasagne missed him because he ducked. She stormed out, and he muttered, 'What did I say?'

How could he have known that the box would open – that as he declared his simple intention to watch the match, her mind would flash back fifteen years and a memory would come flooding back to her. She would remember a man sitting in front of the television, with his meal on a tray. She would see clearly, as though she were there again, a woman trying to share some incident of the day with this man, but he was silent. And she would hear a little girl asking if he would play later and hear the old reply, 'Yes – later.'

Oh, they will make it up, this young couple. And she will say, 'I'm sorry – that was silly.' But it was not silly, for none of us walks through life with the box empty. We each have one, and carry it around with us from encounter to encounter, relationship to relationship – and, of course, into marriage. Sadly, many of us don't even know it's there. All we know is that we seem to react to certain circumstances in a particular way, but we couldn't begin to guess why. The lid is thrown open, and both big and small issues are pulled out – like how we respond to praise, react to a petty argument, or even behave behind the wheel of a car.

That old baggage can drag us down, but it needn't. It is possible to clear some of that old stuff out – to gain insights into the ways we react to situations that are hurtful to those around us. But none of that is easy. It requires patience, understanding and a willingness to change. It means stopping ourselves long enough to ask, '*Why* am I feeling this way? *Why* am I saying these things?' Then we must learn to be honest with our partners about our past hurts, heartbreaks and disappointments. They deserve to know.

Try this exercise. Underline the word which best describes

the home in which you were each brought up. Compare notes with your partner and discuss your answers.

In my childhood home
- We used to make jokes – often / sometimes / rarely
- We used to touch each other – frequently / sometimes / rarely
- Kisses and hugs were – normal / given on special occasions / rare
- When people felt angry, they would – hit out / row / sulk / quickly forgive and forget
- We would discuss our plans – fully / partly / reluctantly
- My business was – everybody's / of interest to the others / my own
- We prided ourselves on our – concern / interest / independence
- In our home, the money was handled by – dad / mum / both
- Nakedness was – accepted / avoided / frowned upon
- Sex was discussed – readily / when necessary / never
- Children were disciplined by – dad / mum / both / never
- Children said prayers with – dad / mum / both / neither
- We had holidays – together / independently / rarely
- My fondest memory of my dad is . . .
- My fondest memory of my mum is . . .
- I was unhappy when . . .

The discussion that comes out of questions like that can be illuminating. Carl and Anne had frequent rows about money. The main difficulty was that Carl couldn't work out why Anne was so fiercely independent with regard to finance. For example, she refused point-blank to have a joint bank account. But as they discussed her past, she related how she recalled watching her mother practically having to beg for housekeeping money each week and still remembers thinking, 'I will never be that powerless.' As soon as they each began to understand why the conflict over money was so strong, they were able to deal with it.

The skill of the lawyer within

Why is it so very hard to resolve conflict? One battle-weary wife posed this question: 'Why do my husband and I find it so hard to resolve our differences? We both seem unable to deal with conflict without rows and major sulking.'

At the heart of this problem is the fact that most of us, in whatever conflict we find ourselves, have an unshakeable belief that we are right.

This came home to me so strongly the other day. I had just had a disagreement with one of my colleagues. It was a pretty simple affair. He said that I had promised to go to a meeting; I maintained that I had agreed to pop in if I could get there. We argued for a while and then parted a little frostily. As I was driving home, my mind was working nineteen to the dozen and I was holding an in-depth post mortem of the whole issue – with myself. 'How could he not remember what I had actually said?' I had a perfect recollection of the exact words I had used. 'Perhaps he *could* remember, and was lying! Perhaps he has just got it in for me. I've got a good mind to tell him . . .'

And then it happened. I'm not sure whether or not to call it a revelation, but certainly I was able to see in a moment why so much of our conflict is so hard to resolve. It concerns lawyers. I am one of those creatures, and it has to do with the way they defend their clients. I have sat in court rooms, listening to the prosecution lawyer saying such awful things about my poor misunderstood client. As he spoke, my client would gasp with surprise and ask me to put his side of the story. 'He was on his way to a fancy dress ball dressed as a burglar and by mistake he entered the wrong house, saw that nobody was in, and was looking through the drawers for an aspirin when the dog leapt on him . . .'

Both lawyers were dealing with the same event, but both seeing it from such different perspectives.

It occurred to me that this is exactly what happens to us in so many of the conflict situations that we have to deal with. We each have what I call an 'inner advocate', a hidden lawyer within, who springs to our defence whenever we enter a conflict situation. This eloquent speaker is determined to present to our mind the best possible case in our favour. He begins by interpreting past events so that we recall them as we want to (that's why both my colleague and I had absolutely clear, and absolutely different, recollections of what was said).

When he has done that, he replays the situation in the best light – for us! We are portrayed as sensible, logical, and gracious – the other party as raving and unreasonable. Finally, he appeals to our emotions and, in an impassioned jury speech, says to us, 'You deserve better than this – look at all you've done for that person' (then follows a quick tour of the last twenty years, with all that they have done for us conveniently forgotten).

When this character really gets going, he is prepared to find other witnesses to support our case – people who will share with us 'in confidence' how they, too, have been badly treated by the villain on the other side.

By the time this inner lawyer takes his seat, we are totally vindicated; the jury have brought in a verdict: 'Innocent!' And all would be well, save for the fact that at that very moment, not very far away, the other person's lawyer is making his closing speech and, incredibly, getting the same verdict. That situation is nowhere illustrated more clearly than in marriage; there the principle of one hundred per cent rightness really comes into its own. He is sure that their financial problems are due to her mismanagement of the household budget: 'If I did the shopping, we'd live on half of what you spend!' She is equally convinced that he is the villain: 'He moans when we spend a fiver on fish and chips, and then goes out and blows ninety pounds on an exercise bike ("for the sake of the kids").' And they *each* wonder in their hearts, 'Has he/she forgotten the long evening we spent last month budgeting, and the promises we made to each other?'

Where there are people, there will be conflict; the important thing is that we should learn how to deal with it.

Basic principles for dealing with conflict

Lose some battles!

One of the reasons why, in some marriages, it is so very difficult to deal with conflict is that one of the partners is good with words and the other is tired of always losing. They have decided that rather than keep coming out of those fights with a bloody nose and feeling as if everything is their fault, they'd rather not fight. And so begins a process where the hurts and frustrations they feel are internalised, and they grow in secret. I have seen the situation where a person is unable to articulate their feelings to their partner and in the end chooses a lawyer to do it. The other person is staggered when their solicitor says, 'Your wife said that you did this, and this and this.' And he retorts, 'She never said a word to me!' And he's right: she didn't – she was tired of losing.

I spend a lot of my life with words, and perhaps you are 'good with words'. But when it comes to conflict, whether it's at work, in the church or at home, the ability always to win the argument can be a positive disadvantage.

We stalk out of the factory canteen, the boardroom, the church committee meeting, or the kitchen, and we've won again. Our brilliant rhetoric has brought us out on top. But have we won? Maybe not. If we could only see into the room that we have just left, and into the emotions of the people there, we would understand why we have lost. There is so much that they needed to say, but they didn't feel articulate enough to do so. Instead, those feelings are trapped in them; but they will not remain trapped for ever, and one day they will come out. And when they do, we would be advised to stand well back.

Winning the argument is often nothing like as important as it appears to be, and some of us need to give the person who is not so good with words the space to share what they feel.

Dianne and I had a row. As I left the house, we were still at it. I was going away that day, and decided I couldn't bear to run a marriage seminar while not talking to my own wife, so I rang her from a motorway service station. It went badly! We started to go over the whole thing again, and then I had a brilliant idea. This would sort it out. It was one of those one-liners that I knew would demolish Di's argument and prove my point. I never got that line out, because for some reason I decided to say the opposite – I just backed right down. The effect on Di was amazing: she changed in her attitude to me; in truth she didn't feel the need to defend her corner any more, because nobody was attacking it! It cost us about two pounds in ten pence pieces just saying, 'No, it was my fault.' 'No, really, it was mine.'

When we deny ourselves the luxury of having to win every argument, one of the positive by-products is that we avoid having arguments over details that don't really matter. In this next conversation, John is the one who normally comes out the winner, and it's Mary who finds it hard even to raise issues, let alone win the ensuing battle.

Scene 1: Kitchen. Mary is at the sink washing up, and John is clearing the table. It's 11 p.m.
Mary (bursting into tears): 'How could you do it! How could you say that about my cooking in front of Mike and Elaine?'
John: 'What have I said now?'

Mary: 'That I'm the only woman you know who can burn water!'

John: 'Mike wasn't there when I said that, only Elaine. You've got it wrong again. He'd gone to get a drink. I know he wasn't there because I remember looking at the clock and thinking . . .'

Mary (pulling out large chunks of hair and beginning to throw the contents of the sink at darling John): 'I don't care where Mike was, and I don't care who was there, and I don't care what time it was, and this is not a court case, and I'm not in the witness box, and . . . you *hurt* me.'

When John launched into his 'let's win on points' exercise, he lost the second he opened his mouth. There was only one way to resolve that conflict – he had to acknowledge that whatever his memory of the events, whatever he had intended or hadn't intended, Mary was hurt, and what it needed was not an argument over the facts, but an apology and a commitment never to speak like that in public again.

As it was, it went back and forth, and finally one of them, in an effort to get out of a tight corner, brought up one of the old memories from years ago, and the hurt lasted a month. The book of Proverbs gives such wise advice here: 'Starting a quarrel is like breaching a dam; so drop the matter before a dispute breaks out'[3] – even if it means losing occasionally!

Let go of the past

There is nothing more draining in a marriage, and more likely to make it hard to handle conflict positively, than a refusal by one of the partners to stop raking up old hurts.

'In our marriage, it seems that whenever we row we both rake up the past. It sometimes feels like a competition to see who can remember the most hurtful things. How can we escape from this?' That is a common and very destructive situation. This couple will eventually tear each other apart.

In today's society, it's a sad but common sight to see a homeless person pushing all his or her worldly goods in a supermarket trolley. The person and the trolley are inseparable. It contains the collection of a lifetime – possessions accumulated over the years – and although perhaps not worth much, they are dearly held.

We have seen a similar sight in some marriages. The husband or wife carries around with them a large sack. But this has in it not precious possessions, but dearly held grievances against their partner – again, built up over the years.

At the very bottom of hers is the memory of how he never did make it to the hospital in time to witness their first child being born. He had stayed at work until the last minute and arrived just too late. Next to that, and nestling in the corner, is the way he treated her mother on that Christmas in 1984. She will never forget how he ruined the whole festive season over a silly row about which television programme they would all watch.

But he has a sack, too, and in it are *his* memories. There's the time she insisted that they go on holiday with that other family. It rained every day (I don't suppose that had been all her fault), but those children had driven him bananas – ruined his whole summer. And then there was the occasion when she refused point blank to go to his office Christmas party. Everybody had said, 'Where's Sally?' and he had murmured, '. . . headache'.

But these old sacks contain more than past hurts; in truth, they contain secret weapons which are brought out every time that battle breaks out.

She normally opens with, 'I will never forget how you . . .' and he counters with, 'Don't talk to me about that; what about when you . . .'

But there's more. Each has, in addition to this normal ammunition, a bazooka. It's a particularly devastating memory, and is only used in conditions of extreme warfare, but, when engaged, it's always devastating. It takes several weeks to recover when you've been hit by one of these.

There are at least two things wrong with carrying sacks like that. Firstly, it's boring. After twenty years of married life, we ought to be able to come up with a few new issues. But the second is more serious; it's that the bag of bitterness will destroy us.

If we are going to give love a chance to grow, we simply have to let go of those old hurts. The Bible calls it forgiveness. It is rarely easy, and it does not wipe out the memory, but it makes the heart promise not to nurse it.

In English law there is the concept of 'spent convictions'. It means that for certain crimes there is a period of time after which they are 'forgotten'. Of course the record of them still exists, but the offender does not have to declare them in every circumstance, for example when applying for a job. In real terms the slate is wiped clean and the person who had been convicted is allowed to start again.

It's vital in our marriages that we set each other free like that, and if we do we will find we have not only liberated our partner, but ourselves as well.

Throwing that old sack of hurts away is something that God has done for us. Corrie Ten Boom put it like this: 'He took all I had done wrong, put it in a deep sea and put up a big sign, "No fishing!"' That may well be the reason that at the centre of Paul's definition of love in 1 Corinthians 13, he has placed the key to it all: 'Love keeps no record of wrongs.'[4]

'Don't speak to me like that!'
So often, it's the way that we raise issues that decides whether we are going to have a sensible conversation or whether World War Three is about to break out. If we say things in an accusing manner, this will generally put the other person on the defensive and, as attack is often seen

as the best form of defence, the stakes are soon raised to full-scale conflict.

If our wife is late home from work, it will generally make her want to hit back if we say, 'Where have you been? You are always doing this to us.' (In rows, we love phrases like, 'you always', 'you never', etc.) The other possibility which will open up the discussion equally well is, 'Thank goodness you're OK. I've been really worried.'

Let me say here and now that I fully understand that it's all very well to write these things, but it is quite a different matter when you have to put them into practice when you are angry. But it's just worth considering which approach has the best chance of successfully resolving conflict.

Laugh it off

Dianne said to me some years ago, 'You know, Rob, life seems so serious these days – we don't seem to laugh as much.' Life *is* serious, and there is so much heartache, but the ability to smile, especially at ourselves, can save us from buckets of tears, especially in the area of conflict. Many rows have disintegrated when one of the partners has seen the funny side of it, started giggling, and finally both have ended up helpless on the floor.

I'm no good at do-it-yourself, but some years ago Dianne insisted that I trim the bottom of a door after a carpet had been laid. I borrowed an electric saw, which went absolutely berserk every time I switched it on. The door was off its hinges, and Dianne was holding it as I tried to perform this tricky operation. We started yelling at each other, giving alternate advice on how to hold doors and use electric saws. Finally, after coming incredibly near to severing one of Dianne's legs, the job was done, but by now the row was in full swing. Then Dianne noticed that I had taken rather a lot off the bottom of the door, and she started laughing. 'Oh well,' she said, 'at least we won't have to get up to let the cat in!' We collapsed in a heap in hysterics! We still look back on that as one of the funniest days of our married life, but it could have been so different. It could easily have been filled with phrases like, 'You're useless; why aren't you like so and so . . .' 'Oh, I'm useless am I? At least I can . . .'

· If we laugh at ourselves, there is great hope for us. I heard the other day of a couple who have named their great fights; it helps them remember not to repeat them, and also to realise how silly some of them were. Among the top ten are: 'The Battle of the Christmas Turkey,' 'The Skirmish at Debenham's Lingerie Counter,' and 'High Noon at Gatwick Airport.'

Ten golden rules for a clean fight

1   Never attack the person for who they are – only what they have done. Instead of, 'You are a useless husband and father' – 'I want us to be a better team together.'

2   Stick to the issue. Imagine that a wife forgets her husband's birthday. He is hurt and needs to say it. But what won't help is, 'You are utterly selfish – you forget everything. The goldfish would still be alive if you weren't so forgetful. Everybody is noticing that you just don't care.'

3   Try not to yell. (But don't feel guilty for an occasional outburst.)

4   Do your best not to interrupt.

5   Remember that if you really love someone, you will spend a good part of your life saying 'sorry' to them.

6   Understand the power of the 'inner lawyer', and ask him to get off your case occasionally.

7   Never fight in public. Having said that, it's not the end of the world for your children to see you rowing, but they need to see a model of how to disagree and how to reconcile. Remember we are creating 'baggage' that they will take into their marriages.

8 Realise that some of our conflict is because we are changing as we get older. Someone has said, 'We are married to several different people in the course of a single marriage.'

9 Really try to understand not just what the other person is saying, but also how they are feeling.

10 Remember the awesome power of forgiveness in both the life of the one who needs it and the one who grants it. As an incentive to forgive, remember that the Bible says that if the Lord kept a record of our wrongs, '. . . who could stand?'[5]

Finally, if this whole chapter doesn't help much, then Richard Erdoes recounts a medieval method of resolving disputes between a husband and wife that you might want to try in an emergency:

> Arguments were settled by physical combat and as women were not as tall as men, the husband was placed at a disadvantage by having to fight from within a hip-deep hole. He was given a club, and his wife a dress with an extra long sleeve, into the end of which a heavy stone had been sewn. If, circling hole and husband carefully, the wife managed to brain her husband, then it was assumed that God was on her side. On the other hand, if the man managed to grab hold of his wife's sleeve, drag her into the pit and subdue her, it was taken as a sign that he had been right all along.[6]

When I read that, I suggested to Di that we might try it as a way of solving our next dispute, but Di with her ever-quick response said, 'No, dear, let's have a change!'

7

Rain in the Desert –
The Power of Appreciation

Many years ago, I was taken by a guide into the Sinai desert.
It was a fascinating journey, and one experience remains as
vivid in my mind as the moment it happened. The guide
stopped the jeep and showed me a very special bush. He
told me that this plant had a rare ability that ensured its
survival in that hostile environment. Quite simply, it had
learnt to live with very little water. When times of drought
came, other vegetation would quickly wither, but this one
died in sections. If no rain came, perhaps half of it would
close down and the rest was able to use whatever moisture
it could find. And then, as the drought progressed, it would
close other parts down, until finally there might be just a
single stem waiting for the rain. And when the rain came,
the seed pods on that stem would explode and send new
life bursting into the desert again.

I have seen the same principle at work in my life and
in the lives of others when it seems that life, faith, and
hope have just dried up and we hang on by the skin of our
teeth and pray that the rain will come again. And I have
seen it in marriage. You can observe it when a man or a
woman becomes starved of self-worth and they crave again
somebody to show them that they matter. This longing is so
deep that if it doesn't come eventually from their partner, it
may be that they will find that appreciation in an affair.

I was sitting in a crowded cafe; on a nearby table, a woman sat alone. As we ate, there was a constant stream of people looking for seats. A man came to the table that she occupied and said, 'Is this place free – are you alone?' She said, 'I'm always alone.' I have tried to imagine what was going on in her life that had made her reach out to a total stranger with such a plea, and such an invitation.

Knowing that we matter

Dr James Dobson set out to identify the reasons for periods of depression in women.[1] He had observed that in counselling sessions with women of varying ages and backgrounds the same frustrations were mentioned. He devised a ten-item questionnaire which listed the themes that had so often been mentioned as the cause of depression. The women were asked to rank the ten items according to their frustration from each source. The most depressing was to be given a 1; the least relevant item scored 10. The participants were married women between the ages of twenty-seven and forty years – the average age was thirty-two. The majority were mothers who still had small children at home. They were asked to fill in the chart anonymously. You might like to try it:

Irritant	Rank
1 Absence of romantic love in my marriage	
2 In-law conflict	
3 Low self-esteem	
4 Problems with the children	
5 Financial difficulties	
6 Loneliness, isolation and boredom	
7 Sexual problems in marriage	
8 Menstrual and physiological problems	
9 Fatigue and time pressure	
10 Ageing	

We have spoken over the past years to tens of thousands of couples on the issue of marriage, had countless conversations, and read and answered hundreds of letters. Having done all of that, I am not surprised at the results of Dr Dobson's survey, because I have seen the same results time after time. The majority of those women chose 'Low self-esteem' as the greatest difficulty in their lives.

Low self-esteem is something that can hit any man, woman or child, and in some it actually becomes a terminal illness. I can best describe it by telling you about a school photograph that made me cry.

It was of a large group of children at the beginning of their teen years. The girls were already looking like women in the making, the boys were looking like – well, large boys. But one girl caught my attention. She was very overweight and sat with her hands on her knees. She did not have a pretty face, but she smiled out from behind thick spectacles. I asked my friend's child to tell me about her.

Apparently, she had few friends because, among other things, she smelt a little and some of the children would not sit by her. She was not good at sport and regularly came somewhere near the bottom of the class in terms of academic achievement. Whenever the teacher asked two leaders to pick teams, she was always the last one chosen, and invariably one captain would say, 'You can have her.'

And as I looked at her, I felt a great emotion well up in me. I wanted to hold her, to tell her that she was wonderful, that she was *somebody*. I wanted to find something in that child's life that she could do moderately well and praise her for it. I wanted to tell her that I would always be her friend, that I would love to sit by her.

In short, I wanted to do for her what our heavenly Father has done for us. He takes people who, if you really knew them, are not very attractive and who, even as adults, crave acceptance, and he says to them, '*I'm for you*. The whole world may be against you, but I'm for you.' He's somebody who gives approval irrespective of physical appearance, academic achievement or sporting prowess, somebody who loves against the odds – somebody who will always sit by you.

That child was like a plant in the desert waiting for the rain, but there seemed no hope that anybody – teacher, friend, perhaps even a parent – would come over the horizon and say, '*I appreciate you*.' As I have recounted that incident at some of our seminars, people have come to me and said something like this: 'I'm forty years old – I have a responsible job – I have three lovely children – but I understand the girl in the photograph – it's how I feel right now.'

As human beings, we need to know that we matter to somebody almost as much as we need breath.

I remember speaking at a church situated on a vast housing estate. The homes were high-rise flats, and it seemed that those responsible for their repair had long since given up. Leaking water ran down the walls, the lifts were broken, and young mums would struggle up the stairs with pushchairs and groceries. Unemployment was high and the suicide rate was rocketing. One woman told me that excrement had been pushed through her letter-box.

It seemed that these people had been abandoned by society and imprisoned in a concrete jungle; as if society had said to them, 'You have no value.' The little church was crowded as I stood to speak, and I began like this: 'However you came into this room – Christian, atheist, agnostic – and however you go out, you are somebody. You have been created in the image of God.' I was saying to them, 'You may feel worthless, but God appreciates you: not for what you own, or the job that you do, but because of who you *are*.'

As I said that, I saw people actually raise their heads. I said the same words recently at one of our marriage seminars, and afterwards a woman came to me and said, 'Tonight has been one of the most important times of my life. I have lived forty years with someone who has made me feel as if I am nobody, but you have told me that in the eyes of

God I have worth. You will never know how that makes me feel.' We crave the knowledge that we matter to somebody.

One of the best-selling management books of all time is a slim volume called *The One Minute Manager*.[2] You can buy it on any railway station for just a few pounds, and yet many employers say that the principles contained in it have revolutionised their workplace. So what great secrets of wisdom lie in the pages of this book that can so change the way that organisations work? It's not difficult. The author says, 'Learn to appreciate people; learn to praise.' He says that if we took just sixty seconds a week to show our appreciation of those who work for us, we would see incredible changes in attitudes, relationships and even productivity. I believe he is right, and I think that way because the principles contained in that book are not new; in fact, they are very old and are contained in a much older book and are based on the fact that we are created in the image of God – that each of us has dignity and we are meant to recognise that in each other. The issue of appreciation, of giving each other worth, is a crucial one in any relationship, but it is rain in the desert to a marriage that is dying.

Over the years we have seen many marriages fall into an ever-deepening spiral of despair. Many things have contributed to that, and for some there comes a time when they say, 'I've had enough; it's over.' But we have sometimes observed a strange thing happen. Something seems suddenly to kick that tired, old, almost dead love into life again. I heard the other day from a couple who were about to have a divorce and yet, for some reason, their attitude to each other began to change and they found love again, stronger than before. Time and time again the ingredient that does this is appreciation. One of the partners decides, almost as an act of the will, to appreciate the other. It is as if they say to themselves, 'I will not go on taking my husband/wife for granted; I will show that I care.' The fascinating thing is that the decision is so often not born out of the emotions, because the *feeling* of love may not be running high, but out of sheer will-power to initiate change. And so they begin in little ways to show that the other person matters, and they find that they have unleashed one of the most powerful agents of change in human relationships: the power of praise – the secret of appreciation.

Mark Twain understood that; he said, 'I can live for two months on a sincere compliment.' In many marriages a partner has to live for thirty years without any real demonstration of appreciation. You can have a home with every labour-saving device imaginable, you can have a prestigious job or the kind of face and figure that make the models on the catwalks look boring, but you will die inside without knowing that you matter to somebody.

What am I worth?

It is fascinating how we evaluate whether we have worth in the eyes of another person – whether or not our partner appreciates us. I once asked Dianne, 'Darling, if you could change anything at all about me, what would it be?' I had rather hoped that Di would have to think about it for a while, but she didn't even hesitate. 'Rob,' she said, 'when you shave, you always leave the stubble around the sink; and I'm not sure how you do it, but you get the shaving foam up the wall – higher than head-height! And when you've finished, you roll the towel into a wet ball and throw it into the bath!' (I was now wondering what was coming next, and had a facial expression which my children call 'gobsmacked'.) Dianne went on: 'I would like you to remove the stubble, and the shaving foam, fold the towel up and put it over the radiator.' I managed to get my jaw back into gear and spluttered, 'Is that it?' Di replied, 'That will do for starters!'

I have thought so much about that incident. Why was that such a big deal to Dianne? I think I know the answer to that now. You see, although Di has had various jobs outside the home, just then she was a full-time homemaker, and she was looking at the devastation in the bathroom and wanting to say something like this to me: 'Rob, just now my job is in this home. When I clean, when I try the picture on this wall instead of that one, when I put things in their right place – that is part of my main task right now. They may seem small things, and be assured there are days when I'd rather be advising the Cabinet on some intricate economic problem. More than that, it's from the job of homemaker that at the moment I get a large chunk of my identity. And when you and the children come home and leave the place as though hurricane Flora has just visited us, it's as if you're saying to me, 'What you do doesn't matter.' And Rob, I sometimes feel that what you're saying is, "What you *are* doesn't matter."'

These may seem such small issues, but if we are to begin to learn the power of appreciation, it's probably at the basics that we need to begin. It is so easy to convey to another person by our everyday attitudes that they don't really matter to us. We came across a moving prayer the other day. It came from the lips of a woman who craves to be somebody in the eyes of those she loves:

Lord, I don't feel loved any more, I don't feel wanted. My children demand so much of me and take it without appreciation. They overlook the things they could do for me and when I ask for their help, they cruelly rebel. My husband is too preoccupied with problems even to suspect this awful vacancy I feel. I scarcely know my neighbours and my friends are too busy with their own concerns to really care.

Who would care, Lord, if I disappeared tomorrow? Who would really care? I know that I am needed, and for that reason alone I would be missed. But wanted, Lord, really wanted as a person, for myself?

You, Lord, you alone know and love and care about me as a person. In you alone I find my understanding and reassurance.

Oh, give us all back reassurance.

Let us feel loved and wanted.[3]

'I find it so hard to show appreciation'

Why do so many of us find it hard to give appreciation and praise? Much of it has to do with taking others for granted. I remember my first bicycle. It had three gears, a saddlebag and *white pedals* (whoever designed a boy's bike with white pedals?). I loved that bike. Whenever I'd finished riding it, I would clean it, making sure that all the rain was dried off and then, when I had finished the frame, I would turn my attention to the pedals. I was determined to keep them 'Persil' white. That kind of attention was a nine-day wonder. Two things conspired to destroy it: first, I just got used to that bike. When it was in the shop window, its very distance made it seem mysterious, but there wasn't much mystery about hitting my leg on it ten times a day as it stood in the little hallway at home. But, secondly, one day I saw Martin Harrison's bike: it had ten gears! Mine seemed a boring old affair by comparison.

So it is in our relationships. We begin with such promise, such excitement, as if our whole married life is to be one great big 'Gold Blend Coffee' advert. And then we begin to get used to each other. It may even be that the things that attracted us now annoy us. What we used to call 'strong' we now call 'stubborn', the gentle personality that had so attracted us we now call 'weak'. Such a taking for granted is a tragedy, and for so many it is not until the marriage is broken and we have lost that person that we begin to realise what good characteristics they had, and how we just got used to them. At the time, it seemed tremendously important that they be thinner, or better around the house, or stronger with the children. But now we remember that they were kind, or warm, that they always had time for us, and we never appreciated it.

Sometimes we find it hard to show appreciation because we have never received it. Many of us have never known a parent's praise. After one of our seminars a middle-aged man came up to me. He told me that he remembers running home from school, having come top in a music exam for the whole of his county. He got ninety-seven per cent. He ran into the house. 'Dad, dad, I came top, I got ninety-seven per cent!' His father said, 'Won't you ever get full marks?' This man was very successful in his career; others looked at him and wished they could be like him, but he represents the many men and women who in adult life are still pursuing the approval of the father or mother they could never please. They may have lived under the shadow of a more clever or athletic brother or sister, and they crave appreciation for what they are in themselves.

Think back for a moment to the little girl in the school photograph. The day may come when she will be a mother. How will she be with her children? Wouldn't you think that she would vow never to put her own children through what she knew? Wouldn't you think that she would resolve never to say to her child in public, 'Hey, look what the cat dragged in,' that she would build her children up at every opportunity? The sadness is that she may well treat her children as she was treated. She never received praise and appreciation, and she may find it hard to give it. And that destructive pattern of behaviour may mean she will never say to her husband, 'I am so proud of you, thank you for what you have done.'

Another reason that many of us find it so hard to praise is because we feel so insecure ourselves. In fact we find it easier to bring others down, as if that very act elevates us. So often that shows itself in the way we talk to our partner. We may delight in criticising them in public or making jokes about their weight or cooking ability. In the home, we may find that we enjoy pointing out where they have gone wrong, or use our tongue as a weapon of destruction.

Destroying self-esteem

Mark and Rachel had known a good marriage. They were in their mid-thirties, had two children and seemed happy. But in reality there was something eating at the heart of this relationship like a cancer. By the time they agreed to counselling, it seemed the marriage was all but over. What had caused that? There were certainly many of the normal problems. They had long since stopped talking to each other. It wasn't that they didn't communicate – they did – but they didn't really say anything. Any in-depth talk about how they really felt was gone. Then there was the busyness that had slowly but systematically choked the love out of this marriage because it stifled it of the one thing it needed to grow: time. There were other common themes that had all played their part in the death of love, but in the middle of them all, one stood out. By no means did it seem at first sight to be the greatest reason, and yet as I listened to them I became convinced that this, above all, had killed the love of that woman for her husband. It was his tongue.

It was a tongue that over the years had been used to bring her down. Sometimes it would be at a party, when it would be a jibe about her weight. If they entertained, it would be a joke about the meal. He would laugh, the guests would smile awkwardly, thinking, 'Why doesn't she throw it over him?' and she would die inside – again.

And that was what had happened; slowly, word by word, over the years of their marriage, he had killed the dignity and the self-worth, the sense of being *somebody* in that woman. And finally, he had put to death the feeling that he was somebody to her.

The Bible is right when it talks about the power of the

tongue. It *is* a 'small part of the body', but 'a great forest is set on fire by a small spark'.[4]

She was in her seventies, had beautiful silvery hair and a lovely dignity about her which made it hard to understand the story that she told me. She had been married twice and she told me that her first husband had killed her love for him with his tongue. She said, 'He would say to me almost every day, "You cow!"' She told me that she took that abuse day after day. She said that single phrase had summed up how he had treated her – as if she were less than a person. And after a while she began to believe it. But then one day, in the middle of another barrage, which again ended with the usual phrase, a thought came to her. She said to herself, 'Cows aren't such bad creatures; you get milk from cows, you get leather from cows, cows are good parents.' The next time he began his abuse, she replied, 'Cows aren't so bad; you get milk from cows, leather from cows; cows are good parents.' And then she turned to me and with a twinkle in her eye said, 'He never called me that again!'

And I have so often seen a husband who feels he is not appreciated. It may be that he says, 'I just bring home the money. Nobody ever says, "Thanks. Thanks dad for the holiday, thanks for the jacket, thank you for all that you do for us." I'm just a meal ticket.' Appreciation is especially vital when unemployment hits a home. I have observed similar symptoms in a man or woman robbed of their job as in bereavement. It is vital at such times that the family let them know they have dignity in the home and are appreciated, irrespective of their ability to bring home money. They must know they are valued for *who they are*.

Six keys to appreciation

1 Create in others a sense of worth
When we show appreciation to anybody, we give them dignity, and it is especially so in the family. We need to

let each other know in a hundred different ways that we are appreciated – that we matter.

My late father used to find it so hard to give praise, but my mother worked overtime at it. Our home was poor; we didn't have luxuries like an inside toilet, or a bathroom, or even running hot water, and I had friends who seemed to be a lot better off, but she gave me something that money cannot buy: a sense of value. Even now, I remember something she said to me in my mid-teens: 'Rob, I know that you have to mix with kids who have more money than we do, but I want you to know that you are as good as anybody; you are not better than others, treat all with respect – but you are special to me and I believe in you. I have saved some money – you and I will call it "the bank" – it's in a tin on top of the landing cupboard. If ever you need money, you must come to me and we will go to the bank together.'

It wasn't until I was twenty-two years old that I discovered that the bank had never existed. How could it? – she had so little money. But she tried so hard to give me, in her way, a sense of value.

It is vital in marriage that we give a sense of dignity to each other.

2 Practise the power of praise

Catch yourself when you are about to give some piece of carping criticism or hurtful comment. I was counselling a couple who, as they spoke, would each bring the other down. At one stage the husband said, 'My wife is obsessed with the thought of our daughter leaving home.' I stopped him and said, 'Try saying that differently. Try saying, "My wife is so concerned about our daughter when she leaves home and how she will cope."' Then I asked the wife to tell me any characteristic in her husband of which she was proud. She mentioned his reliability and utter consistency, and I saw him gaze at her. It had been years since he had heard praise from her lips. They had spent ten years bringing each other down, playing the dignity-destroying game of verbal volleyball. They were experiencing something written in the book of Proverbs by one of the wisest men who ever lived: 'A crushed spirit dries up the bones.'[5] But it was not too late for them to discover the life-changing power of praise.

3 Develop the 'touch of appreciation'

Touch is a powerful tool for conveying to somebody that you appreciate them and give them worth. Some of the most amazing words in the New Testament are spoken of Jesus when he was faced with a leper.[6] The man had the most humiliating of diseases, which prevented him from talking, and even worshipping, with family and friends. In fact, the nearest those who loved him had reached was a few hundred yards as they heard the bell he carried to warn people away. He must have felt he was at the bottom of the pile. And then, 'Jesus touched him.' It may be that the man had not felt a human touch for many years, but here was this young teacher giving him such dignity. Jesus spoke to him, he needed that; he made him well, and he had prayed for that; but before he healed him, Jesus had touched him.

It is so in our families. Meaningful touch is a crucial way of communicating appreciation and love. F.B. Dressler, in 'The Psychology of Touch',[7] maintains that women in particular need eight to ten meaningful touches each day just to maintain emotional and physical health. The role of touch in marriage is often quite different for men and women. Men often associate touch with sex, but a wife will often crave for touch which demonstrates not interest in sexual intercourse, but interest in *her*. A man may say to his wife, 'You never come up to me in the kitchen and put your arms around me any more.' His wife will reply, 'No, because if I do, within five minutes you'll expect me to be diving into bed.' We need to develop touch which does not automatically lead to the bedroom, but which affirms the other person.

The messages that touch gives are at least as powerful as what we say. It could be a father putting his hand on a son's head to convey to him, 'Son, I am so proud of you'; or a wife squeezing a husband's arm as he leaves for a difficult meeting, to say, 'I'm with you in all of this.' It could be that a husband will reach out an arm in bed just to hold his wife. Those simple actions can change our relationships, but, just as with good verbal communication, they don't just happen, and we normally need a little practice!

In our culture, and particularly for men, touch often does not come naturally. It's important, of course, that we find what suits us in our marriage, but it's as well not just to say, 'Oh, I'm not the emotional type!' Touch is powerful, and we need it at all ages. A boy of thirteen said to us recently, 'My parents have stopped hugging me now I'm a teenager, but when nobody else was looking, I wish they still would.' I heard of a woman in her late seventies. She lived alone, and once a week took lessons in ballroom dancing. Somebody asked her if she loved dancing. She said, 'Oh, I enjoy it, but the real reason I go is that it's the only time that anybody touches me.'

4 Find the 'keys to appreciation'
One of the most sobering things about being involved in marriage counselling is to realise how different we all are in our marriage relationships. Some years ago a book was published giving ways to revitalise your marriage. It included tips such as the wife dressing in a skimpy nightie and flinging herself into the husband's arms as he came home from work. The author could never have had children. We can just imagine the romance routine being interrupted by a three-year-old saying, 'Mummy – quick – the cat's got the hamster . . . and why are you dressed for bed?'

The ways that we can express appreciation meaningfully will differ, but in every marriage there will be 'keys to appreciation' – ways in which your partner perceives whether or not you care. Let's say right now that the 'formal' occasions such as birthdays, anniversaries, and Valentine's Day are important, but just as vital is the way that appreciation is expressed in the everyday.

The secret of the 'keys to appreciation' is that these things are important to your partner, not necessarily to you. When Lloyd was very young, I bought him as a Christmas present a very complicated Meccano set. I loved it! In other words, I gave him what I thought he needed. 'Keys to appreciation' are different. They may be small, but they say to our partner, 'I know that this matters to *you*.'

When we hear some of them from the marriages of others, they may sound corny, but they work for them. Let me give you a few of ours. As far as Dianne is concerned, she appreciates flowers and little gifts, and I suppose if I told her that I had booked the Orient Express to take us on a romantic tour with Cliff Richard singing as we went, she'd be grateful. But nothing works like saying, 'Don't do a meal tonight; we'll all get fish and chips – or I'll cook it.' (Kids seen leaving with packed suitcases!) For me, it's when she says, 'Take some time out for yourself – go off for the day – kick the leaves – we'll all try to survive until you get back!' Those moments of personal space say to me, 'My wife cares enough to know I need that time.'

Your keys will be different. It could be not walking past dirty washing on the landing, or helping with some paperwork. These are not world-shattering issues, but they are meaningful in *your* relationship.

Let me give you some I have heard from other marriages:

- Filling the car with petrol and checking the tyres.
- Giving your partner a 'cooking free' day. They don't even have to *think* about food.
- Saying, 'This evening is yours – do with it what you want – I'm holding the fort!'

- Cuddling in bed (without unbridled passion breaking out!).
- Noticing when the house has been 'extra cleaned'.
- Making the bed before leaving for work.
- Saying, 'You go to bed – I'll bring up a drink – get lost in a book.'
- Not passing socks, shoes, or old cups of tea without picking them up.
- Listening – taking the phone off the hook when your partner has something to share that's important to *them*.
- Gritting your teeth and saying, 'Darling, if you want to go there that much, I wouldn't want to miss it for the world.'

5 Take a second look

It's so easy to major on the parts of our partner's character or physical appearance that we don't like. It can sometimes be helpful to take time to consider the positive qualities that we do find attractive. I fully understand that in some marriages the relationship has so broken down that at least one of the partners will say, 'There is absolutely *nothing* that I like about my partner.' The interesting thing is that often after divorce a partner will look back and say, 'I know I didn't love her at the end, but looking back, I can see qualities she had, that if I'm honest, I miss now. It was just so hard to think clearly at the time.'

Take a few minutes to consider some of those qualities. Go on – you may just find something that you appreciate!

- Something my partner has achieved or made that I admire . . .
- Something I like about my partner's appearance . . .
- Something practical I'm glad my partner does really well . . .
- The quality I most like about my partner is . . .
- My partner has put up with me in these areas . . .

6 'Let the good times roll!'

The mind is a fascinating thing. It has the ability to recall events and sometimes block them out. Generally, we look back on the past in a kindly way. That's why, years ago, the summers were always hotter, the Christmases more 'Christmassy', and the policemen more helpful. We can easily fool ourselves if we always wear those rose-tinted spectacles. That's why the book of Ecclesiastes has that fascinating verse: 'Do not say, "Why were the old days better than these?" For it is not wise to ask such questions.'[8]

But the mind can also play an opposite trick on us. When relationships with others are hard, it seems to have the ability to block out the memories of the good times. We forget the time when they stood by us; we cannot recall the years when the relationship was so fulfilling, when we felt so very blessed.

It's a good idea to make a note of moments in our marriage which have been special to us. It could be a holiday, or the experiences learnt together during a child's illness. It may be a little kindness that lifted us when we needed it, or memories of hilarious laughter. It's good to record those occasions, because in times of difficulty we so quickly forget the good things. And it can be at times, when it seems that love has died, and there is no hope for us, that the scanning of those old memories begins the flicker of feeling in us and raises at least the possibility that love could grow again and we could be 'the way we were'.

Take what is helpful in this chapter; use what works for you. But let none of us say, 'Oh, I don't need to say anything or demonstrate by actions – she knows I love her.' That philosophy is a hundred per cent wrong. The only way we can tell if we are valued and loved is by what people say and do. That's why the Bible, which is dedicated to telling us of the love of God for us, is constantly talking about what God has *done* – how he is demonstrating his love: 'Greater love has no-one than this, that he lay down his life for his friends.'[9] Love says, 'This is how much I appreciate you, and even if love seems hard to feel at the moment, then as an act of the will, I will appreciate you.' When we are valued like that, it is life-changing, it affects our very personalities, because it answers the deepest question a man or woman can ask: 'Do I have real worth?'

All that I have tried to say in this chapter is so clearly illustrated in one of my favourite stories. It's from a culture that seems strange to us, but the lesson at the heart of it is universal.

'Johnny Lingo and the Eight-Cow Wife'

It took the sharpest trader on the islands to realise the cheapest deal isn't always the best bargain.

The time I sailed to Kiniwata, an island off the Japanese coast, I took along a notebook. After I got back it was filled with descriptions of the flora and fauna, native customs and costumes. But the only note that still interests me is the one that says: 'Johnny Lingo gave eight cows to Sarita's father.' And I don't need to have it in writing. I'm reminded of it every time I see a woman belittling her husband or a wife withering under her husband's scorn. I want to say to them, 'You should know why Johnny Lingo paid eight cows for his wife.'

Johnny Lingo wasn't exactly his name. But that's what Shenkin, the manager of the guest-house on Kiniwata, called him. Shenkin was from Chicago and had a habit of Americanising the names of the islanders. But Johnny was mentioned by many people in many connections.

If I wanted to spend a few days on the neighbouring island of Nurabandi, Johnny Lingo could put me up. If I wanted to fish, he could show me where the biting was best. If it was pearls I sought, he would bring me the best buys. The people of Kiniwata all spoke highly of Johnny Lingo. Yet when they spoke they smiled, and the smiles were slightly mocking.

'Get Johnny Lingo to help you find what you want and let him do the bargaining,' advised Shenkin. 'Johnny knows how to make a deal.'

'Johnny Lingo!' A boy seated nearby hooted the name and rocked with laughter.

'What's going on?' I demanded. 'Everyone tells me to get in touch with Johnny Lingo, then falls about laughing. Let me in on the joke.'

'Oh, the people like to laugh,' Shenkin said, shrugging. 'Johnny's the brightest, the strongest young man in the islands. And, for his age, the richest.'

'But if he's all you say, what is there to laugh about?'

'Only one thing. Five months ago, at the festival, Johnny came to Kiniwata and found himself a wife. He paid her father eight cows!'

I knew enough about island customs to be impressed. Two or three cows would buy a fair to middling wife, four or five a highly satisfactory one.

'Good Lord!' I said. 'Eight cows! She must have beauty that takes your breath away.'

'She's not ugly,' he conceded and smiled a little. 'But the kindest could only call Sarita plain. Sam Karoo, her father, was afraid she'd be left on his hands.'

'But then he got eight cows for her? Isn't that extraordinary?'

'Never been paid before.'

'Yet you call Johnny's wife plain?'

'I said it would be kindness to call her plain. She was skinny. She walked with her shoulders hunched and her head ducked. She was scared of her own shadow.'

'Well,' I said, 'I guess there's just no accounting for love.'

'True enough,' agreed the man. 'And that's why the villagers grin when they talk about Johnny. They get special satisfaction from the fact that the sharpest trader in the islands was outwitted by dull old Sam Karoo.'

'But how?'

'No one knows and everyone wonders. All the cousins were urging Sam to ask for three cows and hold out for two until he was sure Johnny'd pay only one. Then Johnny came to Sam Karoo and said, 'Father of Sarita, I offer eight cows for your daughter.'

'Eight cows,' I murmured, 'I'd like to meet this Johnny Lingo.'

I wanted fish. I wanted pearls. So the next afternoon I beached my boat at Nurabandi. And I noticed as I asked directions to Johnny's house that his name brought no sly smile to the lips of his fellow Nurabandians. And when I met the slim, serious young man, when he welcomed me with grace to his home, I was glad that from his own people he had respect unmingled with mockery. We sat in his house and talked. Then he asked, 'You come here from Kiniwata?'

'Yes.'

'They speak of me on that island?'

'They say there's nothing I might want that you can't help me get.'

He smiled gently. 'My wife is from Kiniwata.'

'Yes, I know.'

'They speak of her?'

'A little.'

'What do they say?'

'Why, just . . .' The question caught me off balance. 'They told me you were married at festival time.'

'Nothing more?' The curve of his eyebrow told me he knew there had to be more.

'They also say the marriage settlement was eight cows.' I paused. 'They wonder why.'

'They ask that?' his eyes lighted with pleasure. 'Everyone in Kiniwata knows about the eight cows?'

I nodded.

'And in Nurabandi everyone knows it, too.' His chest expanded with satisfaction. 'Always and for ever, when they speak of marriage settlement, it will be remembered that Johnny Lingo paid eight cows for Sarita.'

So that's it, I thought: vanity.

And then I saw her. I watched her enter the room to place flowers on the table. She stood still a moment to smile at the young man beside me. Then she went swiftly out again. She was the most beautiful woman I had ever seen. The lift of her shoulders, the tilt of her chin, the sparkle of her eyes all spelt a pride to which no one could deny her the right.

I turned back to Johnny Lingo and found him looking at me.

'You admire her?' he murmured.

'She . . . she's glorious. But she is not Sarita from Kiniwata,' I said.

'There's only one Sarita. Perhaps she does not look the way they say she looked in Kiniwata.'

'She doesn't. I heard she was plain. They all make fun of you because you let yourself be cheated by Sam Karoo.'

'You think eight cows were too many?' A smile slid over his lips.

'No. But how can she be so different?'

'Do you ever think,' he asked, 'what it must mean to a woman to know that her husband has settled on the lowest price for which she can be bought? And then later, when the women talk, they boast of what their husbands paid for them. One says four cows, another maybe six. How does she feel, the woman who was sold for one or two? This could not happen to my Sarita.'

'Then you did this just to make your wife happy?'

'I wanted Sarita to be happy, yes. But I wanted more than that. You say she is different. This is true. Many things can change a woman. Things that happen inside, things that happen outside. But the thing that matters most is what she thinks about herself. In Kiniwata, Sarita believed she was worth nothing. Now she knows she is worth more than any other woman in the islands.'

'Then you wanted . . .'

'I wanted to marry Sarita. I loved her and no other woman.'

'But . . .' I was close to understanding.

'But,' he finished softly, 'I wanted an eight cow wife.'[10]

8

Rediscovering Sex

The three-year old's room was being decorated and so she had the excitement of sleeping on a camp bed in mum and dad's room. Night came, and to the delight of her father she seemed fast asleep when he and his wife entered their bedroom. They slipped into bed, gave each other a peck on the cheek – and that was when it happened. He suddenly became passionate. She began to protest and the dialogue proceeded in stage whispers:

'No, Samantha will hear.'

'No she won't – she's asleep.'

'Darling, no . . . please, let's go to sleep.'

'How can I go to sleep when you look so ravishing?'

'Unless you've become an owl, that shouldn't be a problem – it's pitch black.'

'Darling, don't do this to me . . .'

'I said, "no!"'

Whereupon a little voice piped up in the darkness: 'Daddy, go to sleep – when mummy says, "No", she means "No!"'

The sexual arena became a no-go area – at least for that night! It's like that for many couples for the majority of their married lives. I don't mean that they never enjoy sex; rather that occasional forays into lovemaking reinforce an idea already held – that they are failures. They have never really clicked in their lovemaking and now it seems that a cold war has set in.

Behind closed doors

As we counsel couples in the area of their marriage relationship, they will often raise in the first interview the issues which they feel are destroying their love. These range from finance to differences over the discipline of children, from lack of communication to untidiness. Sooner or later they will mention their sexual relationship – but as they do, they will bow their heads. Of course, these are personal issues, but it is more than that. It is the belief that 'This is *our* problem. We doubt anybody really understands the difficulties that we experience in the bedroom.'

That sense of isolation is a killer. A church leader rang me some years ago. He shared his deep distress in the seeming failure of the sexual relationship in his marriage, and then he said, 'But I'm the leader of a large church – who can I tell?' I was moved by this man's courage to seek help; but few men do, because so often they believe that nobody else could have gone through a similar experience – nobody would understand. They imagine beginning to share their heart and the other person saying, 'Oh really? How strange . . .'

The sad fact is that many of the so-called 'problems' in this area are not problems at all – they are learning curves. They are no more problems than a toddler falling over as he tries to walk. They have become problems because we have believed that we were the only child in the playground that ever fell over!

It may be that one of the partners was much more interested in sex than the other. That may have caused one of them to feel rejected and the other pressurised – even guilty that they are not 'sexier'. It may be that other elements were introduced into the equation – perhaps the veiled threat of an affair – 'If you don't meet my needs . . .' – or even the subtle offer of sex in exchange for some favour.

What was given as a gift of God has somehow become a source of despair, perhaps bitterness, and may eventually lead to the break-up of the marriage. The tragedy is that this couple love each other. They would love to fulfil each other sexually. The partner who shows less interest is not like that because they want to be; in truth, they don't know why they are like it. They wonder if they are the only person in the world who doesn't thrill at the prospect of sex.

It is especially difficult for such a couple in a society like ours which is dominated by sex. Every soap opera has its sexual adventure, either explicit or suggested. In these romps, the beds are always made, there are never headaches, and energy seems to be as much on tap as the champagne. The magazines are full of articles on 'Great Sex'. To such a couple, these titles only serve to increase the sense of isolation. It's as if a child who hates piano lessons is offered a subscription to 'Play the classics in a week!'

But the real killer is that nobody else seems to have the same problem. Certainly, it seems that other couples are managing. Even if the sex lives of others are not as perfect as one imagines, nobody is talking about the issue, and so for all practical purposes, 'This is just us . . .'

Dianne and I understand that situation so well. In the early years of our marriage our sexual relationship was, to say the least, restrained. In fact, every time I made a move towards her, Di would begin to feel ill. It doesn't do much for your 'macho' image when, plastered with every aftershave you've ever heard of, you slide across the bed in James Bond style, only to have the object of your desire turn green and say, 'Oh, you don't, do you?'

Thankfully, even in those early days, we could talk about these issues. We began to ask ourselves what was going wrong. We came to believe that there were several ingredients which had conspired to make our initial sex life less than newsworthy. Firstly, nobody had ever talked to us about sex in a positive way. Neither of our parents had spoken to us, and in fact, apart from Arthur Harrison drawing me diagrams on the bike-shed wall, we had received precious little instruction. (Thanks, Arthur – you did what you could.)

What information we had gleaned had come from our church background, and I'm sorry to say that it was a hundred per cent negative. We had never heard a church leader talk openly about enjoying sex, and the teaching was limited to warnings:

'Don't go down dark lanes together after the youth fellowship.'

'Don't go babysitting together.'

'Don't sit in the backs of cars together.'

'Don't go around in groups of less than five hundred.'

When I was in my teens and going out with Dianne, an older man took me aside and, in an effort to 'keep you pure', gave me a solemn warning; he screwed up his eyes, and said in a sombre voice: 'What you have to be careful about in sexual intercourse is . . . getting locked.'

I began to stutter, but eventually stumbled out a reply: 'What?'

'Well, it's possible . . .' (eyes darken) 'to get locked.'

'What would happen to us if we got locked?'

'You'd have to go to the hospital to be unlocked.'

I'm sure that I don't have to tell you that the *thought* of Dianne and me sidling down the road to the local casualty department was enough to keep me pure for eternity!

We may smile at how things were years ago, but in many ways little has changed. It's still possible to feel that sex is something less than a gift of God. A woman came to me after a seminar – she was about thirty and had been a Christian for just a year. She told me that her husband, who did not share her faith, had told her that since she had become a Christian their sex life had deteriorated. I was hooked and asked her to explain! She said that until recently they had enjoyed a very full sex life, but that sometimes it was a little unusual. She said that occasionally they would begin kissing on the stairs and end up having sex on the landing. And then she said, 'I realise that now I'm a Christian that's probably not right.' I doubt that anybody had counselled her that sex outside of the bedroom was wrong. It was more likely that she had begun to sense a general unease with sexual issues – and that had affected her freedom. I encouraged her to enjoy sex with her husband – wherever!

There are many people who have been married for years and yet still feel 'dirty' when having sex. I received a letter which said: 'One of the lingering problems in our marriage has been trying to unlearn that modesty has little place in the bedroom – that we can be "naked and unashamed".' That was written not by a young couple just married, but by a doctor married for many years.

Honeymoon disasters

Seeds of future problems can be sown at the very start of a marriage. Last Saturday, thousands of couples were married. For many of them, the experience of honeymoon sex was wonderful; but for countless others it was a disaster. That is true for couples who have slept together before marriage and for those who married as virgins. Many couples feel devastated by what they see as their poor performance, and yet the simple truth is that it's often not an ideal night to have a great sexual experience. One wife, ten years on, remembered her wedding night:

> We were shattered. We'd been up until one the night before putting the finishing touches to dresses, hymn sheets and table decorations. The wedding was lovely – but the reception! I thought to myself, 'If I hear another card read

out, I think I'll explode.' (Anyway, who is Auntie Mary from Tasmania?) And the speeches! By the time we'd listened to everybody in the room recite their favourite bits from 'Great ideas for wedding speeches', it was five o'clock! Don't get me wrong – it was fun getting the tin cans off the back of the car, and finding our cases, but it was tiring. I love Peter more than I can tell you, but by the time we got to the hotel, I was ready for bed – yes, bed!

That is such a common experience. One man came to me at the end of a seminar and told me his story:

I was so looking forward to our wedding night. My wife and I had a meal in the hotel restaurant; while I settled the bill, she went upstairs to our room. I hurriedly paid, shot up the stairs and charged into our bridal suite. She was lying on the bed. I leapt at her. As I was flying through the air, my head hit the light. It started to bleed. In fact we couldn't stop it bleeding all night. We never did have sex . . . we just fell about on the floor laughing.

I have more hope for that marriage than I do for some which begin with an idealistic view of sex.

The tragedy is that many whose early sex life is disappointing often feel so isolated. It is as if they close a door on their marriage in those early months and say to themselves, 'This is our problem – we can tell nobody.' This couple will go through their married life closing other doors. They will be the only ones in their circle of friends who, for a period, don't feel in love; they will think they are the only couple who are experiencing some financial trauma; and they will be convinced that nobody else has the problems with their children that they are facing. These are good people. They will run the youth group and help on the building committee; outwardly, they seem fulfilled – but their hearts are breaking.

I would love to put my arms around them and tell them that it's alright. I would want to tell them of the man who came to Dianne and me and shared with us that it took him and his wife several years to really 'click' in their lovemaking. I would want to tell them to be gentle with each other and to be patient. They could have been helped by so little. Things like this . . .

Sugar and spice . . . and slugs and snails

One day, when our children were small, I disappeared into my study and announced to my family that I was going to write an article about the differences between men and women. One of them looked at me quizzically and said, 'Would my drawing a picture help you?'

There are differences in men and women, both physical and emotional. These are based, among other things, on different brain activity, metabolism and the presence of the menstrual cycle in women. Having said that, I want to stress that it is foolish to say, 'Men always behave like this,' or 'All women react in this way.' As I describe these situations, you may need to interpret them for your marriage. It may be that in your relationship the roles are reversed. What is vital is that we come to an understanding of *ourselves and our partner*.

There are plenty of marriages in which it is the wife who is more interested in sex. Later in the chapter we'll consider the situation where the husband seems to have lost all inclination for lovemaking. Having said that, without question the most frequent comment that we hear on the issue of sex in marriage is from men: 'My wife's not interested in sex.' What is fascinating is to consider what lies behind that situation – why is the wife not interested in sex? The second most frequent comment, which is from women, sheds incredible light on this situation. This comment is usually made in a counselling situation when we ask a couple the following question: 'If you could change anything at all in your married life, what would it be?' Six times out of ten, a husband will reply: 'Sex – I wish my wife were more interested in sex.' And then we turn to the wife. She thinks for a moment, and then says: 'Affection – I wish he were more affectionate.'

Listen to another woman describe how she feels about this issue:

> I love my husband and I believe that he loves me, but he never tells me so. We rarely talk together, now, and although I know that he is very busy, I can't help myself – I resent the fact that he just won't spend time with me. When we go to bed, he often wants sex, but I just can't switch on – I wish I could. He feels that I reject him and I suppose, in a way, I do. It's strange – what I really crave is for him to hold me – just to hold me. The strange thing is, I think if he did that – I'd want sex.'

The following conversation is *typical*, and highlights the kind of difficulty that woman expressed:

Counsellor: 'Tom, what do you consider to be the major difficulty in your marriage?'
Tom: 'My wife's not interested in sex.'
Counsellor, turning to Helen: 'What do you feel is the greatest problem?'
Helen: 'I can best answer that by telling you why I'm not interested in sex. With him, who would be? I've spent an hour making his meal and he comes home and says, "Put it in the oven – I ate lunchtime." He collapses in front of the television and dozes off. When he does wake, it's to yell at the kids or kick the cat. He has nothing to say to me. Then he decides that he has a slight cold and begins sipping bottle after bottle of 'Night Nurse'. It looks as if he's about to go on to richer pastures at any moment,

but from somewhere, he summons the energy to drag himself upstairs and into bed. I come into the bedroom and stand there for a moment, gazing at him. I think to myself, "Well, I've been married to the old boy for twenty years, I'll just slip in next to him and hold his hand as he passes into eternity." And so I climb into bed . . . and suddenly – hey presto – divine healing! I turn to him and say, "You can't possibly want to – you were almost dead a moment ago!" "Oh, I feel a bit perkier now," he says. It makes me feel like a prostitute.'

What is going on in that marriage? Is the wife being used? Yes, she is, but there is more to it than that. With regard to sex, there are two characteristics in which men so often differ from women. This is of course not true of every man, but these characteristics are very common.

Firstly, most men can more easily divorce the act of sexual intercourse from the *total relationship*. For most women, the act of sex is fundamentally linked to the quality of relationship that she enjoys with her husband. A wife wants to know that she is wanted – not just for sex, but to talk with; loved enough to be the recipient of displays of affection which are unrelated to sexual intercourse – and loved enough to be wooed. If a man is uncommunicative and is more interested in the sports page than discussing issues that matter to her, then he had better take the sports page to bed – he's going to have plenty of time to read it. That's why the old advice is true: 'If a man wants a wild Friday night, he had better begin working on it Monday morning.'

Secondly, the speed of sexual motivation. Generally, men respond to sex more quickly. Someone has said that, sexually speaking, most men are like gas cookers – they roar into life pretty quickly and, frankly, they go out pretty fast. Women, on the other hand, are more like electric cookers – they may take longer to warm up, but eventually they're red hot and take longer to cool. After sex, the gas cooker goes out in a moment, but the electric cooker says, 'Hold me . . . talk to me . . .'

Those roles may be reversed – it may be the wife who is more interested in sex and is more easily aroused, but whichever way it is, we need to understand our partner. Men especially need to grasp how vital it is to give their wives displays of affection which are unrelated to sexual intercourse. When we give our partner value, and let them know that they matter to us, we elevate sex, because we enjoy it in a context of mutual esteem, where each believes that they matter and have worth. When we have sex with somebody without valuing them as a person, we debase both them and the act of intercourse. The most extreme example is rape, in which a person effectively says to another, 'I do not know you, and I do not want to know you. I have no respect for you as a person. What I want is your body.' That's why the victim of rape suffers at least two violations – an assault on their body and an attack on their value as a person.

The giving of that dignity may involve many changes in the way that we behave, including the way that we help, support and even speak to each other. It was Walter Trobisch who said:

A woman's greatest erogenous zone is her heart. And nothing touches her heart more than loving and affirming words. Biting, cynical remarks tear holes in the warm mantle of shelteredness which a husband's faithful love gives her. Icy winds then blow through these holes and inwardly she becomes so cold that she cannot respond physically, emotionally, spiritually.'[1]

Resist the pressure to hit a national standard

The most fundamental issue is that couples must find a sex life together that suits them. We are sinking under a weight of expert advice that tells us exactly what we should be doing in our sex lives, where we should do it, and how often. Many of the so-called 'help videos' only serve to make couples feel that they are, sexually speaking, in a remedial class. It's good to read and discuss articles on sex together; it may be helpful to watch a video, but we need to feel secure enough in our relationship to take things at our own pace.

A common question in the letters column of the glossy magazines runs along these lines: 'I have just read that most couples enjoy sexual intercourse approximately 2.7 times per week.' (Don't ask me – I have no idea what the .7 was, either!) 'We don't have sex anything like that often. Have we therefore got a problem?'

It's easy to be intimidated, and even isolated, by statistics that seem to suggest that we're at best inadequate and at worse abnormal. The truth is that the sexual experiences of couples vary tremendously. Some feel deprived if they don't have sex at least three times a week; others are satisfied with once a month. That is not to say that the 'one-a-monthers' wouldn't enjoy, or even want, sex more frequently – it's just that it's not a major issue in their relationship. Sex is important, but it's not the be all and end all of a relationship. The Hollywood stars may well realise that better than anybody. They live in an industry which is dominated by sex. If their screen experience and looks are anything to go by, then their marriages must be full of fabulous sex – but so often those marriages don't last. It almost seems that someone should invent a new proverb here: 'A marriage with sex once a month, where both are satisfied and love each other, is better than a wild six months and then nothing.'

With patience and gentleness, many couples find a level in their sexual life that may not hit the national head-lines, but which suits them.

Finding a mutually satisfying sexual relationship needs a consideration not only of frequency, but of preference.

What does each of the partners enjoy as an expression of sexual love? I once heard of a small boy whose mother had just explained the act of sex to him. His face twisted in disgust: 'And you tell me that they enjoy it? How? Do they eat chocolate while they're doing it?' We are meant to enjoy sex, and that will be helped if we spend time talking with our partner about what they find pleasurable.

When one couple decided, after ten years of marriage, to discuss their sexual relationship, the husband was devastated when his wife said, 'What would really make me feel wonderful is if you'd rub my back.' This dear man had spent a decade rubbing almost everything else in sight, but had never asked his wife what she liked. When he started to rub her back, he wished he could turn the clock back!

It takes time to be able to discuss these issues with our partner, and as we attempt it we should consider two words – honesty and respect. We should be open with each other. There is no need for embarrassment between husband and wife about any of these issues, but there is a fundamental principle that we must respect each other. We do that when we honour our partner's right to decide. If we ignore the feelings of another person, we practise self-dominated sex, which actually destroys love. One wife put it like this: 'I despise the things that my husband makes me do. But he keeps on until I give in – and then I hate myself for it.'

This situation can become almost intolerable where one of the partners is continually fantasising about sex, perhaps after looking at 'soft porn' films or magazines. Some 'experts' say that if it spices up the sex life, who's hurt? The answer is that it is often the other partner who is hurt – unaware that he or she is being compared to this imaginary lover, and not understanding why they can never please their partner. How can they possibly compete with this fictional sexual athlete who never says no, and always looks so attractive? The truth is that sex based on fantasy often leads to less sex, because one of the partners simply cannot bear to be used like that. This inevitably drives the other into further isolation.

It's vital that we spend time considering these issues *together*.

You might like to use the following questionnaire to help you begin a discussion on the issue of sex in *your* marriage.

What do you believe?

- Real intimacy can only be expressed by sexual intercourse.
- The husband should take the lead in lovemaking.
- The husband should be the one to be most knowledgeable about sex.
- Lovemaking is for the bedroom, under the blankets with the light out.
- If we use contraceptives, this should be the wife's responsibility.
- One partner should never deny the other.
- 'Sexy' nightwear is important.
- A couple must always agree about their form of sexual activity.
- An orgasm must be achieved for sex to be successful.
- Tenderness is more important than technique.
- Sex should not be practised when the wife is having a period or is pregnant.
- It can be helpful to read a sex manual together.
- Within marriage, there are no bounds to sexual activity.

If you've just skipped that list, I'd urge you to go back to it sometime – together. It's important to talk those issues through, even if there is a little embarrassment.

The Genesis account of the creation of man and woman is fascinating. If we only read chapter one, we could begin to think that these are two totally different and independent beings – 'Male and female he created them.'² And yet in chapter two of Genesis a lovely balance is given. The curtain is drawn aside and we are allowed to see a little of God's heart in his creation of woman. That account is filled not with difference and independence, but with phrases like 'bone of my bones', 'flesh of my flesh' and 'united to his wife'.[3] When you put those two accounts together, you get something of the mystery of God's creation of man and woman. They each have dignity before God as individuals, and yet in marriage are intrinsically woven into one. Perhaps that is best summed up in the lovely description 'The man and his wife were both naked and they felt no shame.'[4]

Don't try to compete with the media

For many years we have been bombarded with subtle, and not so subtle, messages about the need to achieve in the sexual arena. We are urged to be alluring, energetic and sexually irresistible. Those who are held up as examples are beautiful people who look as if they've never had a headache in their lives, and certainly have never experienced the slightest impediment in perfect sex, time after time. The women are always in perfect health, devoid of all anxiety, never have periods and, of course, are unbelievably slim and attractive. It seems they are able to reach heights of sexual pleasure unknown to lesser mortals.

Then into the arena comes media man. He is wholly knowledgeable, with equipment that always functions perfectly and with performance levels that seem staggering. This couple have sex at least once a day, with each encounter being better than the last and, of course, always culminating in orgasmic crescendos for both.

In the real world, couples walk on to the set of life, not with encounters drafted for them by a scriptwriter, but with their own baggage, experience and information, collected over many years. It may be that their role models were not the ones portrayed by the media, but a mother and father who, it seems, did not love each other and seemingly never enjoyed sex. It may be that one of the partners comes to the marriage having been sexually abused as a child, or perhaps with a belief that sex is somehow 'dirty'.

They not only come with their own 'real' past, but their drama is enacted in the real world – where the participants get tired, and the children get ill and cry at night, and the mind is sometimes preoccupied with worry. In short, it is enacted in a world in which the models are real people.

They were very much in love when they got married. Paul was a hard-working mechanic and Lynette a busy secretary. They enjoyed their life together and shared many activities – including making love. But then there were cutbacks at the business where Paul worked and he had to work longer hours. He came home feeling more and more tired each day. He used to shower and shave when he came home each evening, but now that became too much. Instead, he would eat his meal and, more often than not, fall asleep in front of the television. Lynette felt hurt and angry, but told herself that the situation wouldn't last long, and in any case, the extra money would come in handy – when they had time to enjoy it.

Because Paul was so tired, they made love less frequently, and each time it became more rushed. Although she still loved him, Lynette resented the fact that she seemed to be being used. She felt less and less inclined to be intimate with him when she felt herself touched by oil-ingrained hands and fingers with dirty nails. She became turned off by the smell of his unwashed body and the feel of stubble on what used to be a cleanly shaven chin. The result was that both their appetites for sex were reduced; for each, the reasons were very different. Feeling hurt, rejected and beginning to believe that the marriage was over, Lynette took less care of herself and started to over-eat. She became less attractive to Paul and the feeling of rejection became mutual. They found it impossible to talk about the situation. If they had been able to discuss it, then, with very little change, they could have adapted their lifestyle to meet with their change in circumstances.

It was only when Paul had problems at work that he took the opportunity to speak to the company's welfare officer about his failing marriage. As a result, Paul and Lynette agreed to see a counsellor. They were helped to talk their problems through, to recognise once again their love for each other, and to see what they had allowed to happen. They moved on to regain their individual self-esteem and mutual self-respect and were able to rebuild their love-life, as well as their marriage.

'Time for sex'

The sex lives of many couples would be revolutionised by a consideration of time. We simply cannot develop a deep relationship without creating the space needed for it. So often, the sexual side of a marriage is thought about less than appointments with the dentist, or social evenings with friends. It is assumed that the secret to good sex is spontaneity. There is some truth in that, but if we rely on it, we will be disappointed. One of the major killers of a good sex life together is good old-fashioned tiredness. Most people have sex at the end of the day, but unfortunately that's often the time when energy levels are at their lowest. Someone has said, 'It's like two weak batteries trying to get a spark!'

You may have spent the last three hours struggling with your child's homework, or perhaps entertaining or being involved in a committee meeting (or perhaps all three!). If that's the situation, then it's harder to feel like, let alone enjoy, sex – although it must be said that most men manage to find the inclination, from some deep reserve somewhere! But because women generally take longer to respond to the prospect of sex, tiredness can be a real barrier. So many say,

'When we actually make love, I enjoy it so much, but I rarely feel like it.' Part of the answer is to make opportunity for lovemaking when we don't feel completely shattered.

That will normally involve a little planning. It may be that an evening is set aside. Before we go any further, let me say that I know what's going through your mind – you're thinking, 'I can't imagine anything worse than, "Oh, it's Friday – sex night."' You're right – if it becomes just that. But if it's a night which you have devoted to each other, with the phone off the hook, and in which you can give each other real attention, then you create an environment conducive to *love*making. I have known couples who feel that there's something not quite right about sex at any time other than at night. Apparently, it works as well at eleven in the morning as at midnight.

Taking the issue seriously enough to give it a little planning is half the battle. It is impossible for love to grow, let alone for us to enjoy a fulfilled sex life together, unless we give these goals some real priority. We need to make time, and find the right time *for us*.

Understand that men can lose their sex drive too

We hear a lot about women who are not interested in sex, but more and more often in counselling situations we are faced with a husband who has lost all inclination for intercourse. A couple may have had a good sex life together. In other words, it suited *them*. That doesn't mean that either partner's needs were met all the time, but rather that they found a level which was acceptable. After some years of marriage, it may then be that the husband begins to seem uninterested in lovemaking. At this time, it is crucial that there is real honesty and openness between this couple.

Initially, the situation may go by without comment, but more and more the wife begins to give serious thought to the possible reasons why she is no longer attractive to her husband – why she feels she can't 'turn him on', or what it is that she has said or done to cause such a reaction. As she agonises about the issue, self-doubts begin to emerge, fears grow, and her thoughts may turn to the possibility of there being another woman.

This is often nowhere near the truth. The fact is that her husband is going through a time in his life in which many things seem to be in turmoil, and frequently he will try to sort the situation out *alone*. It may be that pressures at work are affecting him, or perhaps unemployment. It could be that he finds himself in a period of his life where there seems no certainty. He is being overtaken by high-flyers, seems unable to cope financially, and the very process of ageing is wearing him down.

There may be other reasons. It is often said that after the birth of a child a woman may lose her desire for sex for a time. What is mentioned less frequently is that the dynamics of a change in the family can also affect a man in this area. It may be that after the arrival of a child the husband feels his wife is totally wrapped up in the baby. He takes over the role of father, but the role of husband is put aside.

Situations like these can so easily affect the sex drive. He has a desperate need to maintain closeness with his wife, but he is afraid the very intimacy may involve him in a greater input of lovemaking than he feels he can give at this moment. He finds it impossible to share his anxieties. As he finds that he cannot satisfy his wife, he becomes more and more worried about his sex life and begins to doubt what he calls his 'manhood'.

The very worst thing that can happen in this situation is for his wife to pass some disparaging comment about his performance, causing his self-esteem to slip even lower. Rather than risk further loss of face, failure and potential criticism, he isolates himself.

What this man needs more than anything else is to know that he is loved anyway, and that, contrary to much that we hear through the media, sex is not the measure of love. He needs to be able to share what he is going through, and perhaps above all he needs to know that he is not the only man who ever felt like this – it is very common. He may benefit from medical advice or seeing a counsellor, but many men will come through this period of their lives so long as the feeling of isolation is broken and they can talk it through.

Learn to laugh with each other

Sometimes during seminars, people will ask me, 'How can you bear to share such personal details about your marriage in public?' The answer is that most of them aren't personal – they are the experience of the vast majority of the audience. As we talk about our difficulties of communication or conflict, I see on people's faces an expression that says, 'That's just like us!' But when we begin to talk about some of the lessons we have learnt in the sexual arena, I hear sighs of relief that they are not the only ones, and I see them laugh – laughing with us, and at themselves.

Let me share a couple of those 'personal' issues with you.

Firstly, I am amazed how quickly Dianne can fall asleep some nights. She may see a slight twinkle in my eye and say, 'I'm going to bed, darling.' I tear up the stairs about three minutes behind her. By the time I get to the bedroom, Dianne is not only in bed, but fast asleep. I walk noisily, I cough, I put my face right next to hers and whisper, 'I know that you can hear me!' But it's no use, and I sidle into bed, only to hear Di mutter in her sleep, 'Good try, darling.'

Next, I am staggered at how often I misread the signs – even after twenty-three years of married life. It is our anniversary meal. This event has been in the diary for six months, and we have booked a romantic restaurant.

The big night comes – Di looks great, and I am wearing the 'Cliff Richard' sweater she bought me for Christmas and am plastered in an aftershave which guarantees that strange women will give you flowers in the street. It is quite obvious that, for this night at least, I have made myself irresistible.

We get to the restaurant – it is truly romantic. Candles are burning, and in the background someone is playing a Spanish guitar. The fact that their choice of chords is limited to C and G7 can't dull the magic of this moment.

As we are eating, I am thinking, 'Tonight is a certainty.' Gradually, as the thoughts take hold of my mind, I become impatient and say to Di, 'Are you ready for a dessert? Shall I get the bill?'

'Could I just finish the starter, first?' she says patiently. After an eternity, we leave 'El Gringo's' and wend our way home.

Once in the house, Dianne goes upstairs, but I linger a while downstairs and apply liberal splashings of aftershave. Finally I enter the bedroom. She is walking towards me and has on that long winceyette nightdress that she knows I hate. She catches the look in my eye and says, 'Oh, you don't, do you?' 'Well,' I stutter, 'I did think . . .'

The truth is that I didn't need the candles, the guitar or the Spanish atmosphere to get me thinking about sex. I was thinking about it the day we put the date in the diary. That would have been true of most men!

But for Dianne on that evening, the romance was enough in itself. I don't mean the shallow romance, but the real joy of being together in that setting without interruption; without anybody saying, 'There's a call for you,' or, 'Can you speak at . . . ?', or, 'Mummy, where's my shoe?' For Dianne, for that evening (not for every such evening), that was enough in itself. It didn't automatically have to lead to sex. I need to understand that, or I may feel rejected for no good reason. And she, too, must understand it if the shoe is ever on the other foot and it is I who resist . . . (ha, ha!).

As I share the story of that winceyette nightdress, I find that people come up to me and tell me of their equivalent. One church leader told me that his wife had a similar garment; it was long and woolly and dared anyone to approach it. He said that when he left his last church, he stuffed it behind some loose wall boards in his study. About a year ago one of his former colleagues found it and sent it back to them. Isn't it just great to have friends!

These stories are not personal – they are your experiences, and if they are not yours, they belong to the thousands of people we speak to each year. But for so long we have believed that we were the only ones.

Into our home a few years ago came a young couple. Their sexual experience since marriage had been such a source of grief to them. But they came to tell us some good news. They sat nervously, and he said, 'You tell them.' His wife began to tell us of the difficulties that they had experienced, and then said, 'But it has become wonderful.' I asked them what they felt had helped them, and their answer moved me. It was simply that they had heard us share some of the issues that I have talked of in this chapter, including hearing us laugh a little at ourselves, and as they listened a great pressure had been taken from that young couple. She had said to herself, 'I'm not the only woman in the world who sometimes feels so negatively about sex,' and he had thought, 'We're not the only couple going through these experiences – with help, we can get through this.' As their sense of isolation was broken, they were set free to begin to find solutions.

The door of sex in a marriage can be opened again, even if it has been closed for many years. A sixty-five-year-old man told me recently that in the last two years he and his wife of thirty-five years have begun to discover a sexual relationship he had assumed was gone for ever. Many of us will need a little help. It may be a book; some would benefit from professional counselling, others will find that sharing with very close friends – even laughing together – will be a way forward. But for many it will be enough that somebody has taken the lid off this and they have begun to talk together. And all of us would do well to remember that this is *love*making, and therefore it needs more than a little attention – outside the bedroom.

9

Fatal Attraction

One of the biggest box-office successes of recent times has been the film *Fatal Attraction*. It is the story of a man, played by Michael Douglas, who has an affair with a female colleague while the wife he is very much in love with is out of town. I wish every man or woman who is now on the verge of an affair could see it. I believe that in every sense it is a horror film, because it is so very real. Michael Douglas accepts an invitation for a drink after work, but, as somebody said, he might as well have accepted a descent into hell itself. He unleashes unbelievable tragedy on his family, the woman that he sleeps with, and on his own life.

The most frightening part is where we sense that he has lost control. He begins with a little 'innocent' flirtation, no doubt saying to himself what anybody who ever played with an affair has said, 'I can stop this any time I want to.' But he couldn't stop it. There is a phrase in Indian culture: 'Riding the tiger'. The image is of some unfortunate being who finds himself being carried on the back of a man-eating tiger. The animal is speeding along and he desperately wants to get off, but he has a terrible dilemma: if he stays on, he knows that it will eventually end in disaster, but if he gets off, the tiger will eat him. That's the affair.

In our work at CARE for the Family we are often faced with tragedies in family life. It could be the death of a child, or the sudden illness of a spouse, or perhaps a redundancy. These are all events that can have a devastating effect on the life of a family, and yet it seems that to the affair has been reserved the power to inflict such widespread devastation so quickly. A letter I received from the wife of a church leader who had left her for another woman summed that up so powerfully: 'I love him and mourn the loss of my husband, my children's father, our ministry . . . , our home, our income and so much more . . .'

We do well to sympathise with this situation, but if we are to avoid the affair, we need to believe with all our hearts that it could happen to us. The Bible has such wise advice here; it says, 'Let him who thinks he stands take heed lest he fall.'[1]

That is particularly relevant to this issue. The greatest defence against the affair is to know of a certainty that you could be involved in one. Let me repeat this: the affair could happen to you. You may be a loving wife or husband, a fantastic mother or father; you may be so in love with your partner you resent the time spent reading this book because you could be holding hands in the moonlight. But the affair could happen to you. You may be a church leader or a leader in some Christian ministry; you may run marriage preparation classes or be a family counsellor – the affair could happen to you and it could happen to me. And it could happen in the next year.

What price an affair?

You may already have sensed that I feel strongly about this issue. I do! And I feel this for at least three reasons: what it does to the 'innocent' partner; what it does in the lives of children who are involved; and, tragedy of tragedies, the destruction it so often ravages on those to whom it has promised so much. The affair is well-practised at leaving everybody broken. All of these reasons are encapsulated in the following account:

Some time ago I was asked to spend some time with a man whom I had not met since school days. He had heard that I was now involved in trying to help hurting families, and said that he desperately needed to see me. As he came towards me in the hotel foyer, he forced a smile, but soon he was pouring out his deep tragedy. He had been married for just over twelve years and had 'a wonderful wife and two fantastic children – aged eight and twelve'. He told me that life seemed to be going well for them all, until his employers asked him to take on a temporary assignment that meant he had to stay away during the week. It wasn't long before he had become attracted to a younger woman who worked at the same office, and a few months later they began an affair. For a while he kept this from his wife and family, travelling home at weekends to be with them; but then one day his wife discovered what was happening, and he had to make a choice. He decided to leave his wife and family and move in with his lover. The week before he met me she had decided that she didn't want to stay with him and had walked out. He cried in front of me and said, 'Rob, I have lost everything I ever valued, and yet I cannot stop thinking about that other woman.'

Here was a man who had so much, yet for what he described as 'a few months of fun' it was all written off. I wonder if you have any sympathy for him? I do. I can understand what happened to that man; each of us is vulnerable. Having said this, my real sympathy lies with his wife and children. By his own words, she was a 'fantastic wife and mother'. And the bitterness that now pours out of the letters he gets from her solicitor is the only defence she's got for an ego that's been knocked for six. She feels at times less than a woman.

This is a side of the affair that is rarely shown in the films, where it is so often glamorised. In real affairs, there are men and women who don't want to live any more because they feel the very foundation of their lives has been taken away.

Yes, I have sympathy for that woman, and I also have sympathy for those children. They had rights too. In the society in which we live, many circumstances may deny a child of a mother and a father, and I know what a fantastic job many lone parents are doing. But I know the children of this marriage needn't have been robbed of that right. This couple had put in twelve years with those children. When they were very small, they had got up at nights to comfort them; they had seen them off on the first day at school; they had bandaged cut knees and, as their children entered the teenage years, they needed to be around to bandage broken hearts. For twelve years, they had done all that, and they had another twelve to go, and then some more. But those few 'months of fun' put an end to it all. The price that the affair exacted from that man was so very high, but it didn't leave it there: it called on a wife and two children to pay their dues as well.

It's not fashionable to talk about the 'cost' of an affair. The current mode is to talk about 'personal freedom', to emphasise that we have a right above all else to be happy. I do not believe that we have that right, irrespective of the cost to others. I see too much personal pain on a daily basis to talk about this lightly. These are not easy issues, but none of us can survive any relationship, including marriage, if we first think about what is good for us. Every day of the year, another four hundred children are affected by the break-up of their parents' marriage.[2] These aren't just statistics, they are people with names.

One of those statistics has a name – 'Emma'. When she went to school this morning, Emma went without a kiss from her father. She is just six and had no way of knowing that yesterday's kiss was the last. She may well be one of the fifty per cent of such children who within two years will never see their father again.[3] If we are going to love against the odds, we have to consider those we have promised to love.

Listen to this little girl's account. She wrote it as a woman, but she remembers word for word a conversation that took place in the hallway of her home as her father left:

'Darling,' he said, 'I know it's been bad for you these past few days and I don't want to make it worse, but there's something I have to tell you. Your mum and I are getting a divorce.'

'But dad!'

'I know you don't want this, but it has to be done. Your mum and I don't get along like we used to. I'm already packed. In fact, I have to catch a plane that's leaving shortly.'

'But dad, why do you have to leave?'

'Well, darling, your mum and I can't live together any longer.'

'I know that, but why do you have to leave our town?'

'Well, I've got somebody else waiting for me, now.'

'Dad, will I ever see you again?'

'Of course you will, darling, we'll work something out.'

'But what? You'll be living away and I'll be here!'

'Maybe your mum will agree to your spending a few weeks with me in the summer and perhaps two in the winter.'

'Why not more often?'

'I don't even think she'll agree to that, darling, much less more.'

'Daddy, it can't hurt to try.'

'I know, but we'll have to work it out later. Now look, my plane leaves soon and I've got to get to the airport. I'm going to get my luggage. I want you to go to your room so you don't have to watch me – and no long goodbyes, either.'

'OK, daddy, goodbye. Don't forget to write to me.'

'I won't. Goodbye. Now, go to your room.'

'Daddy, I don't want you to go!'

'I know, but I have to.'

'Why?'

'You wouldn't understand.'

'Yes, I would!'

'No you wouldn't.'

'Oh well, goodbye.'

'Goodbye. Now go to your room. Hurry up, now.'

'OK. Well, daddy, I guess that's the way life goes, sometimes.'

'Yes, darling, that's the way life goes . . . sometimes.'

She said that after her father walked out of the door, she never saw him again.[4]

Come with me, if you will, to a park near your home. Look down the path and you will see a young family. The mother and father each hold the hand of a toddler; they are teaching him to take his first steps. At times he's practically suspended, but that doesn't bother them: their child is beginning to walk. I want you to imagine we could interrupt that little family and that the child could talk to us as an adult. He looks at us and says, 'I am trying hard to learn to walk into this world that you have brought me into. What can you promise me if I succeed?'

What will our answer be? We can't promise him a job – successive governments have been unable to do that. We can't promise him peace – no child of any generation has been assured of that; the difference is that this child will live all his life on the edge of a holocaust. Of course we can't promise him he will always be safe; in fact we can't even promise he can walk home from school free from danger.

I can imagine this child looking up at us and saying, 'I am struggling hard to learn to walk into a world like this. What can you promise me? Can you promise me that you who have brought me into this world will see me through all of this – together?' We say, 'No, we can't promise you that, but we can promise you a computer by the time you're six, a TV in your bedroom by the time you're ten. We'll give you a little device so you won't even have to get out of bed to change channels. We'll give you a personal stereo and a CD . . .' And then our heads go down because, in reality, we can promise him so very little.

It is not uncommon to hear of a couple who are experiencing problems in their relationship, and someone will say, 'They're staying together for the sake of the children.' I'm not so naïve as to believe that is always the right course, but I have to tell you that I believe it's a good reason. And I know countless couples who decided to do just that, and who found their love again in the process.

It is often so difficult to love against the odds. There are times in almost every marriage when the affair seems very attractive. We imagine it and dream of the excitement and the sense of freedom it will bring. We would do well to recall some words of George Bernard Shaw: 'There are two great tragedies in life. One is not to get the desire of your heart – and the other is to get it.'

It's not uncommon for us to speak to somebody at the beginning of an affair. They will say something like this: 'I feel alive again. I feel as if I am truly free. I doubt that I ever really loved my husband. Don't think that Andrew broke our marriage up – it was over long before that. I am in love for the first time in my life.' I don't doubt those emotions. But the truth is that it's not hard for the affair to impress. By its very nature it *is* exciting, with its ingredients of the secret rendezvous, fascinating conversations and wonderful sex. But the promised happiness of the affair is so often an illusion. And I know that because I often speak to those same people two years down the road, and they say, as a man did to me recently, 'I have been a fool. I believed I would be free, but I am in prison.'

Are there affairs in which those involved live happily ever after? I'm sure that there are, but I haven't met one yet where it wasn't bought at tremendous cost to somebody, and I've known many where at least one of the partners wonders whether it was all worthwhile.

Who's to blame?

'Last year, my husband had an affair. Friends sympathise, but they say that I must have done something wrong. I confess I wasn't perfect, and there are things I would change now, but do I have to go on bearing some responsibility for what happened?' Those words are filled with sorrow, and while I believe the advice of that woman's friends *may* have been correct, there is no guarantee that it was. There are so many kinds of affairs.

There is the kind that Ian fell into in the Christmas of 1987. He was a middle manager at a printing plant where he had worked for ten years. He had been married to Kathy for eight years and they had two children: Joshua, aged six, and Kirsty, aged four. To all who looked on, they had a happy marriage.

The office party started with a meal at 8 p.m. It was a fun event, and all the more so because it had been decided not to invite partners. In any event, as somebody had pointed out, 'They would have been bored stiff with all the office talk.' When the meal was over, it was almost twelve. As Ian got up to leave, somebody suggested moving on to a club for an hour or so. He began to refuse, but then several people pressed him – after all, this was Christmas. He was going to ring Kathy, but then thought, 'I'll stay for ten minutes and then leave – she'd only worry.'

When he entered the club, it was like going back to his teenage days. He had almost forgotten how dark, loud and noisy these places are. Somebody bought him a drink and then somebody else grabbed him by the arm, and soon he was dancing. Ian was no dancer, but he managed to last out two of the faster numbers and was glad when the pace dropped a little. The woman that he had been dancing with came closer and he held her. This was brilliant. He felt nineteen, and he was sure that, although he had now long gone past events that he could share with Kathy, it was all under control.

They danced a while longer, and left the club together at two o'clock. He offered to take her to her flat. The sex, when it came, was brief, awkward and unfulfilling, and he drove home in a daze. Kathy was awake when he got in, but in fact she didn't say a thing. She didn't have to – he knew that his face told it all. She just got up quietly and went into the guest bedroom. If he could have rolled time back and died as he entered that club, he would have. He cried himself to sleep. He couldn't have been more repentant. He offered to leave and said he'd understand if she ended it all then. But she didn't: she tried with all her heart to forgive him. It wasn't easy; they went through a year of what she described as 'a kind of dying', and then they began to rebuild their trust. They are still together, and love each other more than ever.

The affair that Jane had was different. It first came to light when David found a cufflink in the car. He told himself that he was silly to be concerned, and yet she had been so distant lately. He mentioned it to her when she came home. She hit the roof. She had always been loyal, she said – how could he hurt her so much? He felt guilty for even mentioning it – and such a fool.

And then, three months later, he was at the school sports-day and Hannah's mother said, 'How was Bournemouth?' He fumbled for an answer and saw the woman redden and blurt out, 'My husband has never met you, but he knows Jane and thought he saw you together. I'm sure he was mistaken.'

But the very worst was when he rang a mutual friend. 'Sian, is Jane having an affair?' 'Of course she is, everybody knows it.' And everybody did. Their friends knew, and the people at her office knew, but he didn't know. For two years it had gone on – late nights at the office, broken-down cars, weekend sales-conferences, coded calls that were now so pathetically obvious. His wife was having an affair – it had happened to them.

I mention these two cases because I want to say that I believe it's wrong when people discuss affairs and say something like this: 'I know that he/she has done wrong, but in the affair there are never truly innocent partners. They wouldn't have had an affair if everything had been alright in the marriage.'

I believe that often there are 'innocent' partners. I believe that Kathy and David were 'innocent'. I do not mean by this that those people were the perfect husband or wife, or that there was nothing they couldn't have changed about the way in which they related to their partner. I mean that they had done nothing to deserve the affair. In fact, affairs occur in marriages which are good, but which are maybe going through a difficult period. They even occur in marriages which are blissfully happy, but where one of the partners has suddenly, and often with bitter regret, had a 'one-night stand'.

The tragedy about the affair is that it has the ability to make everybody feel responsible for it – except the people who are involved in it. It's not at all uncommon to hear children say, 'If we'd been better behaved, dad wouldn't have gone'; or to hear a husband or wife torment themselves about their past mistakes. Having said that, there are situations in our marriages in which we can act in such a way as to make our partner more vulnerable to the affair.

149

Books have been written on how to have an affair-proof marriage. I have reservations about such advice. It implies that if you follow a certain strategy, your marriage will be safe from the affair. The problem with that is that it deals with only one kind of affair, the kind that is born out of dissatisfaction and yearns for experiences long since gone within the husband-and-wife relationship. But there are other kinds of affairs, and these can hit any marriage. They are not necessarily built on things which have gone wrong in the past. The key to avoiding them is to understand their nature and to see them coming.

The difference between those two types of affair is the difference between the charge of the Light Brigade and Pearl Harbor. Both of these were disasters of military history. Both had incredibly tragic consequences, but for quite different reasons. The charge of the Light Brigade, although brave, was foolish. The cavalry went storming into a valley, and we know the situation well:

> Cannon to right of them
> Cannon to left of them,
> Cannon in front of them.
>
> . . .
>
> Into the jaws of death,
> Into the mouth of Hell
> Rode the six hundred.[5]

An onlooker wouldn't have had to be an expert in military strategy to have been able to prophesy the result. Some affairs are like that. When they occur, friends and relatives say, 'We knew it; it was bound to happen – he didn't spend time with her'; or, 'She took him for granted.' The couple had treated each other in such a way that disaster was almost inevitable.

Pearl Harbor was different. The American navy didn't go looking for trouble – trouble came looking for them. Their downfall was not that they couldn't have defended themselves, it was that they just didn't think attack was possible.

If you go searching for an affair, you will surely find one. The tragedy is that you may not go looking, but the affair will find you. Ninety per cent of the defence in such circumstances is to understand what is going on. The charge of the Light Brigade – where we can see danger coming; and Pearl Harbor – where it hits us out of the blue. We'll consider both kinds of affair in the next chapter.

10

The Heart of the Affair

One of the most basic needs of human beings is to believe they matter to somebody. Fifteen years ago, a man who had been practically sleeping rough came to share a Christmas meal with us. He was thirty-three years old and had spent most of his early life in children's homes. As we sat around the table, some friends gave him a few small gifts. He began to cry. Dianne suggested that he stay with us that night. He has never left us.

When Ron had lived with us for a short while, he got a job as a dustman. I was anxious that he got to work on time, so I used to get up early to take him. One evening I got in from work and Ron was leaning back in a chair with a big grin on his face. I asked him what was so funny, and he explained. 'Rob,' he said, 'when you drop me off at work, the other men in the yard ask me, "Who is that who brings you to work in the car?" and I tell them, "Oh, that's my solicitor!"'

I have thought so much about that. Ron had never had a mother to take him to infants' school, had never known a father ask him how his first day at the comprehensive had gone. And what was important to him was not my job or the car, but that he mattered enough for somebody to take him to work. He was experiencing as an adult what he had never known as a child. I have seen him change so much over the years; he has a new dignity and he has given us so much. I pray that he will never leave us. He knows he matters to somebody.

The belief that we matter to our partner is vital in marriage. That belief begins to die when we perceive that we are being taken for granted. The tragedy is that the craving to be wanted is so strong that it leads many who feel they have lost it in marriage to look for it in the affair.

Each marriage is different, and there will be many and varied ways of expressing to our partner that they are valued. But if these expressions of worth are missing, we lay our marriage open to the affair. When we take our partner for granted and fail to give them a sense that they matter, we should also take it for granted that somebody else may do the job for us.

In *Straight Talk to Men and their Wives*, Dr James Dobson cites the following letter as typical:

John and I were deeply in love when we got married. We struggled for the first two or three years of marriage, especially with financial problems, but then he got a promotion that requires him to work long hours; we need the money. He's so tired when he gets home, I can hear his feet dragging as he approaches the porch. I've so much to tell him, but he doesn't feel like talking. I make his meal and he eats it alone. After his meal, he makes a few phone calls. I like to hear him on the phone, just to hear his voice. Then he watches television for a couple of hours and goes to bed, except on Tuesday night, he plays basketball or sometimes there's a meeting at the office. Every Saturday morning, he plays golf with three of his friends; on Sunday we're in church most of the day. There are times when we go for a month or more without having a real in-depth conversation. I get so lonely in the house with the kids crawling all over me. There are no other women in our neighbourhood I can talk to. I honestly believe he's never had a romantic thought, there's no closeness or warmth between us, yet he wants to have sex with me at the end of the day and there we are, lying in bed, having had no communication between us in months. Yet he expects me to be passionate and responsive. I tell you, I cannot do it. Sure, I go along with my duties as a wife, but when the two minute trip is over and John is asleep, I lie there resenting him; I feel like a prostitute. Can you believe that? I feel used for having sex with my own husband, that depresses me. My self-esteem is rock bottom right now, I feel that nobody loves me. I'm a lousy mother and a terrible wife. Sometimes, I think probably God doesn't love me, either.[1]

That scene is set for an affair. For this woman, the main attraction of the affair will not be sexual; rather, it will be the yearning to be valued. She is more likely to fall into an affair when she meets a man who makes her feel like a woman again – who gives her dignity. He may say 'Please give me your opinion of this,' or 'Say that again – it was fascinating.' He may comment on her clothes or hair. It is not that this woman is a star-struck teenager angling for compliments, but she is longing to know that she still has significance *as a woman*.

They came up to me after a seminar. They were in their mid-forties and had obviously both been crying. He had his arm around his wife, and he said, 'For the first time today, I understand that my wife's affair wasn't all her fault.'

The need to be valued

I have never heard the craving for worth illustrated as clearly as in the following poem. It is over a hundred years old and was written by a woman to her husband to explain why she had an affair. The last line has in it the phrase 'the statutory cause', which refers to the use of the plea of adultery as a ground of divorce:

Branded and blackened by my own misdeeds,
I stand before you not as one who pleads

For mercy or forgiveness, but as one,
After a wrong is done
Who seeks the why and wherefore.
Go with me,
Back to those early years of love, and see
Just where our paths diverged. You must recall
Competitors and rivals, till at last
You bound me sure and fast
With vow and ring.
I was the central thing
In all the universe for you just then.
Just then for me there were no other men.
I cared
Only for tasks and pleasures that you shared.
Such happy, happy days. You wearied first.
I will not say you wearied, but a thirst
For conquest and achievement in man's realm
Left love's barque with no pilot at the helm.
The money madness and the keen desire
To outstrip others, set your heart on fire.
Into the growing conflagration went
Romance and sentiment.
Abroad you were a man of parts and power –
Your double dower
Of brawn and brains gave you a leader's place;
At home you were dull, tired, and commonplace.
You housed me, fed, clothed me, you were kind;
But oh, so blind, so blind.
You could not, would not, see my woman's need
Of small attentions and gave no heed
When I complained of loneliness; you said
'A man must think about his daily bread
And not waste time in empty social life –
He leaves that sort of duty to his wife
And pays her bills, and lets her have her way,
And feels she should be satisfied.'

Each day,
Our lives that had been one life at the start,
Farther and farther seemed to drift apart.
Dead was the old romance of man and maid.
Your talk was all of politics and trade.
Your work, your club, the mad pursuit of gold
Absorbed your thoughts. Your duty kiss felt cold
Upon my lips. Life lost its zest, its thrill
Until
One fateful day when earth seemed very dull
It suddenly grew bright and beautiful.
I spoke a little, and he listened much;
There was attention in his eyes, and such
A note of comradeship in his low tone
I felt no more alone.
There was a kindly interest in his air;
He spoke about the way I dressed my hair.
And praised the gown I wore.
It seemed a thousand, thousand years and more,
Since I had been so noticed. Had mine ear
Been used to compliments year after year,
If I had heard you speak
As this man spoke, I had not been so weak.
The innocent beginning
Of all my sinning
Was just the woman's craving to be brought
Into the inner shrine of some man's thought.
You held me there, as sweetheart and as bride;
And then as wife, you left me far outside.
So far, so far, you could not hear me call;
You might, you should, have saved me from my fall.
I was not bad, just lonely, that was all.
A man should offer something to replace
The sweet adventure of the lover's chase
Which ends with marriage. Love's neglected laws
Pave pathways for the 'Statutory cause'.[2]

We live in a culture where it is so easy for people to feel devalued, and we need to fight against reinforcing that in marriage. Society says to so many women, even today, 'What you do doesn't matter.' It is especially true of the young mum at home with small children. It is so easy for her to believe that she has no value. It's all summed up in the question they get asked at parties: 'Do you work?' I've some sympathy with the mum of three children, who said:

Yes, I do work. I'm in a programme of social development. At the moment, I'm working with three age groups. First of all, toddlers; that involves a basic grasp of medicine and child psychology. Next, I'm working with teenagers; I confess the programme is not going too well in that area. Then, on evenings and weekends, I work with a man aged thirty-nine, who's exhibiting all the classic symptoms of mid-life crisis. That's mainly psychiatric work. The whole job involves intricate planning, excellent administration, and a working knowledge of basic theology. I used to be an international fashion model . . . but I got bored!

Paul penned some incredible words in his letter to the Ephesian Christians. He wrote against a backcloth where you could divorce a woman for putting too much salt on your food, or speaking too loudly in public, or for saying nasty things about your parents; a woman was a chattel, a thing that was owned. Against that dark background, he wrote these radical words: 'Husbands, love your wives, just as Christ loved the church.'[3] That kind of love is the opposite of taking somebody for granted. We are meant, above all, to demonstrate in marriage that we matter to each other.

Mid-life and the affair

Being taken for granted is something that can affect a man as easily as a woman. And it can especially happen in the mid-life years. This is the time when so many men fall into an affair. He's a loving husband and father, he runs the local youth football team, he is always willing to help; he's a salt-of-the-earth man. But there comes a time for him when he suddenly feels as if the bars have come down, and he's caged. He looks at his job, his wife, his children and asks, 'What does it all mean?' A word often on his lips is 'bored', although it's deeper than that.

It's as if he can see life slipping by. He may have been passed over at work, or have known the trauma of unemployment; it may be that he now realises that his dreams will never be fulfilled. He sees his body ageing. The television advertisements scream at him, 'This is a young man's world.'

One of the less sociable games my children love to play whenever we're in a shopping precinct is 'Spot the "LCT"!' It means 'last-chance trendy'. These middle-aged men wear a uniform. They normally have a short leather jacket, with a shirt undone to the midriff, and a chest medallion. The outfit is always topped off with white shoes! I can tell you I understand how that man feels. He is trying to hold on to a little youth. The ageing process is so hard to deal with. Henry Still sums it up like this:

There comes a day, perhaps a chill, damp dawn in autumn, when it's more difficult to spring out of bed and face the work of the world. You feel a twinge of stiffness in the knee or shoulder. Dry skin flakes when you scratch. Sitting on the edge of the bed, you're reluctant to meet the day and you contemplate blue veins in the ankle or calf. There's a brown pigment spot on the back of your hand. There's been a change in the weather, you note absently, signalled by the soreness in the pink slash scar where the gallbladder came out last year. Dawn provides a moment to wonder how high your blood pressure is, and how your cholesterol level is doing. You can't quite remember what it was you told yourself last night not to forget this morning. A bathroom mirror is cruel at dawn. It reveals a roll of fat around the body, loose skin under the chin, and grey in the stubble before the lather goes on.[4]

At such a time, a man may begin to ask questions that his teenage children are asking: 'What's it all about? Where am I going? What do I want out of life? What am I accomplishing?' There is nothing wrong with these questions, except he also begins to question things he has never doubted. 'Do I love my wife? Do I want to continue my responsibilities as a father? Do I want to go on doing the job I have?' And as youth looks forward and old age back, he looks at the present and asks, 'What can life give me now?'

Such a man may go through a period of depression, or perhaps cynicism; a man who has had a lovely generous heart suddenly becomes critical of anybody and anything in sight. And sometimes such a man will fall into an affair.

I see that man so often. He has a lovely wife and family, a good job, and a life that others may envy, but he is restless. He fears that if he waits too long it will be too late for him to break out of the rut he feels he is in. There is a tremendous temptation to 'have a little fun' with a younger woman, 'while there is still time'. Such a man doesn't have to wait long to find an opportunity for his dreams of an affair to turn into reality.

And for a while the affair is all that it promised to be. In short, he is having fun: 'For the first time in twelve years, I am doing things that I want to do. I'm not carrying the shopping or hassling with the kids over whose turn it is to clean the rabbit hutch or trying to renegotiate the payments on the mortgage. I am having fun!' And it *is* fun for a while. Their love nest is protected from the hassles that hit any ordinary marriage. His bank manager doesn't have the address, nor does the children's headmaster, nor even the local vicar. There are no garages to clean out on Saturdays, or children to run to Cubs or piano lessons. The sex is wonderful, the conversation electric, and the sense of enjoyment undeniable.

And then a strange thing happens. It all settles down to normality. The taps in the new house had seemed as if they would never leak but, sure enough, there it is – that old dripping sound that used to drive him crazy in the kitchen at home. The letter box had seemingly been programmed not to allow any bills to pass, but now they tumble in – just like they did at home. The conversation is not quite as stimulating; the sex is still good, but life's about more than sex. This man is acting out the truth of Dr James Dobson's immortal words concerning the affair: 'The other man's grass may be greener, but it still needs mowing!'

The tragedy is that what he responded to first was somebody taking an interest in him. Of course sex was a part of the attraction, but as important may be the need to be wanted, even desired. It is so easy for the new woman in his life; all she has to think about is, 'What does he need and can I give it to him?' She may not be as physically attractive as his own wife, and others may look and say, 'I wonder what he sees in her?' But that's the wrong question. He is with her because of what *she sees in him*. She tells him how much he is needed, how he is appreciated, even desired.

Ask any mistress. Her man doesn't do anything but talk endlessly. Mistresses are experts in the art of listening. People think a mistress has a sexual manual that keeps a man bewitched, but actually what she really has is the capacity to listen. (Melissa Sands, founder of Mistresses Anonymous.)

What Melissa Sands says about men is also true of women. Many a woman has begun an affair when she met a man who listened. Why is listening such a big deal? The answer is that when we listen we give our partner value. The alternative is to go on taking them for granted, and that kills love. 'Look at him,' she says, 'boring old him, in his striped pyjamas and brown slippers.' But she is staggered when 'boring old him' is found to be so attractive to that younger woman. 'Look at you,' he says, 'why don't you smarten yourself up a bit?' She does, he doesn't notice – but somebody else does – and he's devastated to get the note pinned to the fridge door – she's gone.

The affair flourishes in an environment where a person feels that they have no real significance, where they believe they don't matter to anybody. The affair says to that person, 'Your wife/husband may not be interested in you, but I am; in your job, you may have been overlooked, but I value you. You may feel that you are no longer attractive, but I find you attractive.'

Part of the power of the affair is that it can impress *so very easily*. If you want to impress your marriage partner, you have to do it over many years, but the affair can dazzle in a moment and seems to have the ability to make those involved in it suspend any rational thought. Husband, wife, children, friends, careers, all count for little in the light of this new relationship. It enables those involved in it to forget all the hard lessons learnt, and it whispers in their ear, 'It will be different with me.' That's why that old line still works, 'Your husband may not understand you, but I understand you.'

Let's face it, the world of marriage is often not conducive to keeping romantic fires burning. Life is so busy and there are so many things to attend to. Children get ill, hamsters get lost, garden walls fall down, and we just get used to each other. If we are to love against the odds, it will mean that we try harder to understand our partner, work more intensely to fulfil their needs, and occasionally surprise them.

That sense of surprise fights against getting into a rut. Women, if you're ever bored around Christmas time, stand at the lingerie counter at Marks & Spencer's and watch men buying nightwear for the women in their lives. Their eyes are wide, they are so excited that when they do make a choice they can scarcely write the cheque. They take this little thing home (and it normally *is* a little thing) and put it in a box with a bow on it. All their greatest hopes and wildest dreams are contained in that little box. They hand it over on Christmas morning and watch your face as you open it. I don't know what they hope for; perhaps they expect you to jump straight into it and drag them by their hair up the stairs. But no, you open it and say, 'Oh, how lovely, just what I wanted.' You are really thinking, 'More pressure, more guilt; I can do without this – it can go with the other twenty-seven in my drawer.' Women, let me say this: if this is such a big deal to him, climb into the thing occasionally and surprise him. He'll probably have a heart attack anyway!

We will help defend our marriages when we give value to each other – when we stop taking each other for granted. The key to doing that is to remember that what most of us want above all else is to know that we matter. When we continually strive to give each other a sense of worth we build a wall around our marriage that will help us resist the snare of infidelity. If we don't consider these issues, then like the Light Brigade we charge into the cannon without a thought. But even if we do all that, we may still have to face Pearl Harbor and the situation where the affair comes looking for us.

The 'Ten-second Rule'

Over the years, I have talked with many men and women who have been involved in affairs. One of the most salutary things is to realise that many of them didn't intend to be unfaithful to their partners. They sometimes blurt out, 'It just happened.' They will normally go on to talk about some innocent event in which they were involved (often a genuine desire to help the other person in some way), and then go on to say, 'It suddenly got out of hand.' I believe it is vital for us to understand how some affairs progress; and just to show that there is nothing new under the sun, I'd like us to go back three thousand years.

One of the most sobering stories in the Bible concerns King David. Ask any Jewish person today about that man – he will tell you of the greatest king that Israel ever had. Ask any man or woman in the street to name their favourite portion of the Bible, and the chances are that they'll choose the poem that this man wrote, 'The Lord is my shepherd . . .' – the twenty-third Psalm. The Bible describes David as a man 'after God's own heart'.[5] Now take a moment to read about David's 'Pearl Harbor':

> In the spring, at the time when kings go off to war, David sent Joab out with the king's men . . . But David remained in Jerusalem.
>
> One evening David got up from his bed and walked around on the roof of the palace. From the roof he saw a woman bathing. The woman was very beautiful, and David sent someone to find out about her. The man said, 'Isn't this Bathsheba, . . . the wife of Uriah the Hittite?' Then David sent messengers to get her. She came to him, and he slept with her . . . Then she went back home. The woman conceived and sent word to David, saying, 'I am pregnant.'[6]

'. . . but David remained in Jerusalem.' David had fought so many battles, and had won most of them. He had overcome Goliath, and songs had been written about his fighting ability. But David decided to sit this one out. And he was wandering around on the roof of his palace. Some have felt that, frankly, David was a little bored. But bored or not, he wasn't looking for trouble, and certainly not looking for an affair – just loafing around waiting for some news of the battle. And then he saw her. She was one of the most beautiful women he had ever seen, and she was naked – his eye had stumbled across a woman bathing.

The rest of the story reads like some best-selling fiction. He invites her back to his place, sleeps with her, and then he gets the news, 'I'm pregnant.' Her husband was out of town at the time – fighting for King David. And then David seems to lose all sense of reason and embarks on a strategy of deceit and, ultimately, murder.

The big question is, 'When did David fall into that affair?' Did he fall when he invited Bathsheba back to the palace, or when he climbed into bed with her? Was it really all over when he began to deceive Uriah, or when he had him killed? No! I believe that David fell in the ten seconds after he saw this beautiful woman and kept on looking. For David, by then, it was all over.

When is the battle won or lost in the office affair? Is it decided at the bedroom door? No. The battle is so often decided when somebody smiles at you across a room and you have ten seconds to decide whether you will walk those twenty feet or keep talking to the boring colleague next to you. There is, in so many affairs, a line that has to be crossed. The tragedy is that so often it is drawn very near the beginning of the relationship, but once it is crossed, it's hard to go back. I spoke recently with a man who was in the middle of an affair. He had lost just about everything. He said to me: 'Rob, she offered me a lift. The second I got in that car, it was as if it was all decided.'

Next Monday morning, in a town near you, a boss will ring his secretary and will invite her to have lunch. It will be an 'innocent' business lunch. And they'll meet the Friday after that, and the week after, too. After a few weeks, the lunches will get longer, but he'll say, 'It's OK, we can make the time up – I'm enjoying talking to you.' And soon they will begin to enact a tired old soap opera, with lines so corny you would hardly believe them. But he'll say something like,

'You know, my wife doesn't really understand me.' And she'll reply 'I think I understand you.' Or she'll say, 'Peter never notices what I wear – he wouldn't notice if I came out naked.' 'I notice what you wear,' he'll say. 'That's new, isn't it?' And the following Friday they'll sleep together.

When was that battle lost? It was decided in the ten seconds after the thought crossed his mind to invite her for lunch. There was a short time when his hand hovered over that phone – he knew where it could lead, and it would have been relatively easy to have backed off then. And for her, it was decided in the ten seconds after the invitation and she had to make up her mind. By the first lunch, they had crossed the line. It wasn't so much that they were looking for the affair, but the affair had found them.

It is sobering to consider the pain that could be saved – to husbands, wives, friends, and little children – in those ten seconds.

After one of our seminars, a man wrote to me:

> Rob, as you spoke of the power of the ten-second rule, I wanted to stand up and yell, 'Listen to him – he's right!'
>
> I fell in those brief moments. My wife and I are together again now, but when I think of the tragedy I could have saved others in those ten seconds, I want to weep.

You can ignore the ten-second rule and still pull back, but it's harder. In truth, the tiger is picking up speed – and you're on its back.

Ten Defences Against the Affair

1 Know when you are vulnerable

I visited Israel for the first time almost twenty years ago. I have been back several times since, but it is a memory from that first trip that is most engrained in my mind. It is of the mountain which tradition says is the site of one of the temptations of Christ.[7] Whether or not it is the authentic site others must judge, but when I saw it it was shrouded in mist and I could easily imagine that scene twenty centuries ago. That particular battle against temptation was won, but I believe there are lessons there which give us indications of when we are worth tempting.

Christ was alone. We are so very vulnerable when we are alone. We may be surrounded by people. We may have jobs where others crave to be with us or seek our opinion, we may live very active lives; but at the deepest levels we are alone. There is nobody we can talk to on a personal level, nobody with whom we can take the mask off. That is tragic, because the Bible is so honest about its heroes – every one of them men and women with feet of clay, who were able to serve God not because of what they were, but so often *in spite of what they were*.

I understand that we cannot wear our hearts on our sleeves with everybody, but we each need one person or a small circle of people we can be open with. These people can warn us, encourage us, and above all save us from the vulnerability of isolation. Some will say that all of this is meant to be found within marriage, but if that were true then the Bible would only encourage single people to 'carry each other's burdens'.[8] Men in particular need other men with whom they can talk in depth. Many women have two or even three friends with whom they will share the most intimate details of their lives – most men don't have one.

2 *Know yourself*

Fifty per cent of avoiding the affair is understanding when we are vulnerable. When Christ was tempted, he was physically exhausted. He had not eaten for forty days; all his body's natural reserves were at an all-time low. There come times in many of our busy lives when we are physically shattered. It happened to the Old Testament prophet Elijah. He had fought many battles, but there came a time when

he lay under a tree and said, 'I have had enough, Lord
... Take my life.'[9] One man, now reconciled with his wife,
when asked what contributed to the affair in his life, said
'I was desperately weary in spirit and body.'

3 Resist the temptation to prove that you are still irresistible

What a temptation it is to prove that we are still attractive.
We may be enjoying an intriguing conversation which is
completely 'innocent' (even if we are thinking, 'If I have
to hold my stomach in for five more seconds I am going to
die!'). But there comes a moment when we realise we
may be playing with fire. It's then that we need to walk
away. It is relatively easy to do it then, but so very hard
later. The power of the ten-second rule is awesome.

4 Keep the romantic fires alive within marriage

Fight against taking each other for granted, and hear each
other's calls for help. Build into your marriage defences
against the affair. Build each other up, never bring each
other down in public. Instead, give to each other the precious
dignity of worth – that we are somebody.

5 Understand the illusion of the affair

The affair promises so much, but so very often delivers so
little. The trick of the affair is to offer us all that we feel we
may have lost in the past – in a moment – as if in a capsule.
It says to us, 'You deserve better.' Sheer self-pity has led
many men and women into affairs. But the real tragedy
for so many is that the affair robs them of whatever joy
and dignity they did once possess.

6 Be careful whose shoulder you cry on

Avoid discussing your marriage problems with anybody who
may misinterpret your motives or take advantage of you. It
is just asking for trouble to say to somebody of the opposite

sex, 'John and I are going through a tough period at the moment.'

7 Guard your eyes

Christ was so incisive when he spoke in the New Testament about the possibility of committing adultery with the eye.[10] In our society, it is very hard to stop giving the eyes more than enough to cope with in terms of infidelity. With the advent of the 'in-room film' service, there are hotels in our country which are little better than sleazy cinemas, with at least fifty per cent of the films on offer being soft pornography. That is not just an insult to women, but conspires to make it harder for the man away from home to be faithful. We so often want what we see; our partner, by comparison, seems dull and uninteresting; it makes it harder to win the battle.

8 Learn to run

When the ten-second rule is long since blown and you know you're in trouble, then run without dignity and without poise.

9 Understand the cost

If we could only go to the end of our lives and see it all in perspective, we would change so many of our actions. If we could just see where they were all leading; but the affair doesn't normally allow that vision. Instead, it says to us, 'Trust me for tonight – tomorrow's another day.'

One eight-year-old boy put the whole thing in context. He said, 'My dad doesn't love my mum any more and he's found someone else. But he doesn't know how sad we are – 'cos I know that if he did, he would never have left us.'

10 Believe in the power of forgiveness

For some who are reading this chapter, this is not just an interesting topic, it is a searing memory. Some mornings they wake with it in the pit of their stomachs. For the sake of these people, I would never have written the last two chapters unless I could have written the next. And that is so because not just in the affair, but in a thousand other circumstances – and especially in marriage – we will never be able to love against the odds unless we can give and receive the incredible power of forgiveness.

11

Dealing with the Past – The Freedom of Forgiveness

Hollywood loves to give accolades. There are awards for 'best picture', 'best actor', best supporting actor', and many more. But if there's ever a a prize for 'most inaccurate comment concerning relationships' then that, too, will go to Hollywood. It was uttered during a film that in the Sixties caught the imagination of a generation. The film was *Love Story*, and the phrase was 'Love means never having to say you're sorry.' Anybody who has ever spent more than a day with another human being knows that the opposite is true. Love is *always* having to say you're sorry.

People hurt each other. We do this because at times we're selfish or foolish or insensitive – sometimes all three at once. And the old song is true, 'You always hurt the one you love.' That doesn't mean we don't hurt those we don't love; it is simply an observation, that so often we reserve our deepest hurts for those who matter to us most – or at least for those to whom *we* matter most.

For all those reasons, the only hope for us as we try to love against the odds – try to love those who hurt us, wound our spirit, or rob us of dignity or hope – is that we forgive them. This forgiveness may be for small hurts, or for years of somebody breaking our heart.

Sometimes those who spend their lives showing patience and kindness to others seem to run out of it in their own home. Peter is an orthopaedic surgeon dedicated to working with children. He has to show incredible gentleness in his job, but with his own family he found it harder:

As long as I can remember, I've struggled with a personal problem that would surprise most of my friends and colleagues – anger. I'm not talking about temper tantrums in the operating room or fits of rage at medical associates when they make mistakes. At work, I'm a pretty easy guy with whom to get along.

At home, well, the record's not so clean. From time to time, somebody will push my button the wrong way, usually not even deliberately, and without much warning they end up with a rather loud earful from me.

My wife, Cathie, has been as patient and understanding about this as anyone could be. I'm sure she's prayed many times that I would overcome this dark aspect of my personality . . . Not long ago, I thought that I had it beaten. When I came home, I informed Cathie that she was seeing the new me.

A few weeks later, the new me announced my intentions to spend quite a lot of money on something that I wanted to use with our two sons for recreation. Instead of arguing with me, or even trying to reason with me, Cathie just gave me *one of those looks* . . . the kind that used to flick my fury switch. Unfortunately, it still worked.

I slammed the cupboard door and then basically withdrew into myself. I wasn't about to say anything to her. The silent treatment continued through Sunday night and all day Monday. By Monday night, the surgeon's old nature was aching for a fight and, this time, my wife was more than willing. We blew up at each other, shouting – screaming would be more accurate – like we never had before.

Ridiculous as it sounds now, I went into our bathroom and sat there on the floor, thinking, *Now why won't she just come in here and say she's sorry? Then we can stop this foolishness.* Evidently, however, she was thinking something similar, because we went to bed that night without a word.

The next morning my car was in for service, so Cathie drove me to work in stony silence . . .

That day, I had . . . one of the most complex operations I've ever had. The case took all day. Since I had to wait for Cath to come and pick me up, I had some time to kill. Anticipating this, I had taken my Bible with me, along with the homework for our couples' Bible study that evening.

We had been studying Ephesians for some time, but I wasn't quite prepared for the supernatural one-two punch about to come my way when I opened my Bible to our text, Ephesians 4:25–32: '. . . Do not let the sun go down while you are still angry. And do not give the Devil a foothold . . . Get rid of all bitterness, rage and anger . . . Be kind and compassionate to one another, forgiving each other just as in Christ, God forgave you.'

If ever I doubted it before, I then knew that God has a sense of humour. *Here is what you need to know*, He said, *and here is what you need to do.* That evening Cath and I forgave each other and then had a good laugh about it.[1]

'Cath and I forgave each other.' The awesome power of forgiveness is that it allows you to take something that might have grown like a cancer until it destroyed – and deal with it. It was forgiveness which allowed this couple to cut through the pain and hurt. Without forgiveness, but with time, the memory of the conflict may have faded a little and life have got back to a semblance of normality. But the problem with that is that the hurt is buried, not dealt with.

A few years ago, somebody not too far from our home was having some building work done in their garden. It involved the use of heavy machinery. As one of the large diggers tore at the ground, it unearthed a skeleton. A murder inquiry was started. Whoever buried that body must have gasped if they saw the evening news that night. They had believed the old wrong was buried for ever. Hurts which are not dealt with can be like that. You can submerge them in some far corner of your mind, but watch how quickly you can find them when you're hurt the next time. And that's where forgiveness comes in – it allows you to take a hurt in all its ugliness and to say quite clearly, 'You hurt me more than you will ever know . . . but I forgive you.' When forgiveness is in operation, it releases two sets of people – the one who has done the wrong from the guilt of it and, just as important, the one who has been wronged from the need to nurse it.

Forgiveness is hard!

Forgiveness is the breath of Christianity. That's why it's tragic that although in many of our churches we have sermons on forgiveness, can buy books on forgiveness and sing hymns about it, when the crunch comes we find it so hard to forgive. I remember being asked to speak to a group of churches. I mentioned that forgiveness is the hallmark of the faith and that if we cannot forgive each other then we have no right to try to share our faith with a broken world. When I had finished speaking, the chairman pointed me to a group of people huddled together in conversation at the back of the church. He said, 'It's a miracle – they haven't spoken to each other for ten years.'

Somebody has highlighted why we find it so hard to forgive others. It is because we have no idea of how much God is prepared to forgive us: 'Our churches are full of nice, kind loving people who have never known the despair of guilt . . . or the breathless wonder of forgiveness.'

It's often so hard to forgive. We say to ourselves, 'Nobody should be asked to forgive what I have been through.' And yet the reason we are asked to forgive is because God forgives us.

How important is your reputation to you? I have sat in courts and heard the reputations of innocent people dragged through the mud. I have seen the hurt in their faces at the injustices that were being piled upon them. It happened in another court room: a trial in which Jesus was in the dock, the witnesses lied, and where they took a reputation and rubbished it.

How important is your body to you? What if you were taken, as some are even today, hooded, beaten and humiliated? What if they put nails in your hands and feet and pinned you to a piece of wood – as they did to his body on that Friday?

And how important is your spirit to you? What if, at the time you most needed to be in contact with your heavenly Father, they laid something on your shoulders that caused you to cry out in the darkness, 'My God, my God, why have you forsaken me?'[2]

How important are they to you – your reputation, your body and your spirit? What did he say? 'Father, forgive them, for they do not know what they are doing.'[3]

You may say, 'I know all that, but I'm not Jesus.' Nevertheless, we are meant to reproduce the forgiveness that we have received from God, and to show it to others. This is why at the heart of the prayer that Christ gave we find, 'Forgive us our wrongs, as we forgive those who wrong us.'[4]

This is the heart of it – that God is willing to forgive us. There is in Luke's gospel an account of a very unusual party. It wasn't unusual because a prostitute came to it – prostitutes often to go parties – it was strange because of forgiveness.[5]

Jesus had been invited to the home of one of the religious leaders where there was a party going on. Let's try to imagine what went on . . .

As the guests arrived, Simon, the host, would have stood at the door and kissed each one – it was a sign of welcome.

Then the slave would bend and wash their feet, and, finally, the host would take a little oil and put it on the guest's forehead – it said, 'Friend, you are welcome in my home.' And all those things happened to every guest except the young carpenter. He was not kissed, and the slave was told to leave his feet dirty, and he was not anointed with the oil of welcome.

In the village was a prostitute, but Jesus had changed her life. She heard that he was at the party, and she longed to be near him. Outsiders were allowed to sit on the fringes of such occasions, and she made her way to stand near the little stone shelf that surrounded the room.

The guests ate as the Romans used to, lying on couches or sometimes kneeling, but either way the unwashed feet of Jesus were showing. She must have been standing right behind him because, as she saw these indignities poured on the one who had so changed her life, she began to cry. (Luther called those tears 'heart water'.) And the tears hit the dirty feet of Jesus. Then she did something no woman of repute would have done in public – she undid her hair, let it fall, and began to dry his feet with it.

The religious men, some of whom were no doubt taking an excessive interest in the menu card as they saw her come in, had no difficulty in interpreting this little scene. In short they said, 'He's nobody special – if he were, he wouldn't let her touch him.'

And then it happened. The young teacher turned to the woman at his feet and said words that brought the roof down on that party – words that still rang in her ears when she was an old woman, words that seemed somehow to undo the chains of the past. He said, 'I forgive you.'

After the words, 'I love you,' the most needful words any human being needs to hear are, 'I forgive you.' That is true whether we are married or single, rich or poor, male or female. We need to know we are loved, and we need to know we are forgiven.

Forgiveness and the affair

If this is true anywhere, then it is true in marriage. It is impossible to love against the odds without forgiveness. But it is often in marriage that it is hardest to forgive, and that is especially so in the affair.

The letter that remains uppermost in my mind in recent years was from a wife and mother. It has stayed with me partly because it is so very ordinary. The events that she described occur in many marriages, but as I read her account I sensed that hidden in this letter was hope, and that the secret of hope was forgiveness:

Dear Rob, on Saturday my husband and I attended the Marriage Matters seminar. It was a day that changed our lives. In the morning, before leaving our home, I said to my husband, 'I think this seminar is our last hope; if nothing good comes of this day, I think we may have to part.' You see, after fourteen years of marriage, he had an affair. I've not been able to forgive him; however sorry he said he was, I simply could not. That was until Saturday. But when you spoke of God forgiving us, I thought, how can I not forgive? And your words made me think so much about my children, my little girl and my little boy; they deserve a happy life, a mother and a father to love and to care for them. The whole day made us look at our family, and we talked so much that night, and we're still talking. We laughed a lot, and at the end of the day we cried together. Thank you. Saturday changed our lives – we're both looking forward to a happier, brighter and more loving life together. Here's to the next fourteen years.

Forgiveness was not easy for that woman to give, and maybe not easy for her husband to accept. I also understand that it does not wipe out the past, or mean that she will never wake again with that familiar knot in her stomach. Forgiveness is not created in Disney World. It does not say, 'What you did didn't hurt me.' Forgiveness says 'What you did hurt me more than you will ever know, but I will no longer hold that against you – I want us to begin again.'

Forgiveness at this level is an act of courage and faith. It is courageous because we often do not want to forgive – we have been so hurt, our very spirit seems to demand retribution. We also know that we are committing ourselves to show that we are trying to put the past aside, and we know how hard it will be.

And it is an act of faith, because we know we may be hurt again.

Can we ever trust again?

A few years ago I was putting my notes together after one of our seminars. The auditorium was empty – but not quite. As I lifted my head, I saw a young couple, probably in their early twenties, standing near the platform. They seemed as if they had so much they wanted to say, but just weren't sure that they could say it. Eventually they stepped forward, and he began to tell me their story.

He told me that about a year ago he'd had an affair. It had rocked their young marriage and he had been filled with remorse. He said, 'After it happened, I took my wedding ring off, and gave it to my wife, and asked her not to put it back on my finger until she could trust me again.' He then lifted his hand and, smiling, said, 'Last month, she put the ring back on.' I turned to look at the young woman, who stood with her head bowed; she seemed, somehow, not to be part of this celebration, I said to the husband, 'Please forgive me if I have got this wrong, but I think that when she put that ring back on your finger, she was not saying, "I trust you again" – she was saying, "With all my heart, I *want* to trust you again."' As I said that, she lifted her head and said, 'Yes, that's how I feel.'

You see, forgiveness could not say, 'What you have done didn't hurt me.' It couldn't even say, 'It never happened – I trust you as much now as ever I did.' Trust would take years to build again. No, forgiveness is not magical, and yet it can make such a difference because it has both a spiritual and a practical dimension. First it says, 'I will not hold the wrong that you have done against you. I release you from it.' It is therefore an act of the spirit. But it is also a practical act. It also says, 'I will never remind you of this, and so far as is possible, I will forget it.'

Sometimes we love to nurse our hurts, to pull them out in front of friends like some old war wound and say, 'Do you remember what she did to me? Oh, I've forgiven it, but things can never be the same again.' That is not forgiveness. Forgiveness strives so that, as far as is possible, with all our human limitations, things *can be the same again*.

But even with forgiveness we must tread carefully and with sensitivity. Very often in the affair, the partner who has hurt the other will ask for forgiveness. Their partner will give it, but it seems that then a problem comes. The partner who has been forgiven expects everything to return to normal overnight. He cannot understand why she may find sex difficult for a while, and he resents it when he is late home and she asks him where he has been. Perhaps he will say, 'You still don't trust me. You haven't really forgiven me because you still remember.' And there is the answer. God forgives and forgets, but we cannot always forget so quickly. Somebody who had struggled with this pain said, 'You never realise what a good memory you've got until you try with all your heart to forget something.'

Forgiveness in action

The wonder of forgiveness is that as we begin to let go of the hurt, God can heal the wound. We desperately need families in which the members are used to saying sorry to each other – where there is an atmosphere of forgiveness.

Archibald Hart is Dean of the Graduate School of Psychology at Fuller Theological Seminary, California. In his book *Overcoming Anxiety* he talks of helping to free our children from over-anxiety. The advice that he gives in this area has so much to say to us about the way we need to forgive as adults:

Always provide a forgiving home. To prevent anxiety, parents must guard against creating excessive guilt feelings in their children. Discipline is essential for children. But all discipline must have an element of forgiveness built into it. Whenever an act of discipline is invoked, there must be a clear message that the misbehaviour has been forgiven.

To a young child feeling guilt for his misbehaviour, discipline isn't enough. What he craves above all else is freedom from his guilt feelings. After all, what's the point of discipline if it doesn't restore our fellowship and love?

It's not enough to say, 'Oh, she knows I've forgiven her because I don't bear grudges.' Children need to hear and feel the forgiveness. First, we can say it. It is better to say 'You are forgiven' – including God and whoever else is involved in the forgiveness – rather than 'I have forgiven you.'

The other way we can show forgiveness is to demonstrate it. Try to show through every word and deed that follows that your forgiveness is real.

Every act of forgiveness you demonstrate after you have disciplined your child is a precious gift to him or her. With these gifts, your child can build happiness and freedom from debilitating anxiety. I guarantee it.

The following elements are crucial:

1 **Create a home which has an atmosphere of forgiveness.**

2 **Deal with the conflict.**

3 **Say 'You are forgiven.'**

4 **Demonstrate that forgiveness.**[6]

There is a crucial question here that can't be ducked: 'Can I forgive somebody who is not sorry for what they have done?' I believe there are circumstances in life when we can forgive those who have wronged us, even if they seem not to regret what they have done. We release them from the debt to us – and we leave judgement to God. Many who have done that experience a feeling of release, as gradually bitterness and resentment begin to fade. It is as if *they* are set free.

The sad thing about this is that the person who has done the wrong doesn't enjoy that forgiveness – it's hard for the relationship to be rebuilt when they can't even acknowledge their wrong. If the power of forgiveness is to bring *mutual* healing, then it needs to operate with first of all genuine sorrow on the part of the one who has done wrong, and then absolute forgiveness by the one who has been hurt. Anything less tends to be whitewash through which the cracks soon appear.

This is not to say that after forgiveness life is plain sailing. In truth, forgiveness is something that needs to be in our hands and hearts every day – both to give and to receive. There is no greater power on earth, no attribute with a better ability to change lives, than the act of forgiveness.

They brought her to Jesus – the woman caught in the

act of adultery – pulled her, it seems, from the very bed. She stood there with just a blanket covering her. Wherever was the man? The religious ones threw her at the feet of the young teacher.[7] Listen in to the conversation:

'We have rules, and by our rules she should die. We should stone her.'

'Then do it – but let the one who has never done wrong throw the first stone.'

And then he bent and began to write in the sand. The men began to consider what he had said, their eyes alternating between the broken woman and the pile of stones. As his words burnt in their spirits, they began to walk away, beginning with the oldest. The truth is, the older we are the more we know how vulnerable we are. But eventually, even the young men went – just threw down the stones and left.

And then he lifted his head to her.

'Where are your accusers?'

'There are none left, master.'

'Then neither do I condemn you – go, and sin no more.'

To know that forgiveness is an incredible freedom. It is the heart of the cross of Christ. I have often thought about the thieves who died either side of the young carpenter that day. One of them joins in with the crowd as they mock the figure next to him. The other defends him, and then turns and says, 'Jesus, remember me when you come into your kingdom.' The reply he got has echoed down two thousand years: 'Today you will be with me in paradise.'[8] Strange that Jesus knew it would be 'today' – sometimes it took days to die on a cross; wonderful, the promise to 'be with me', but best of all was the implication that said, 'Every wrong that pins you to your cross – I forgive.'

The power of his forgiveness is not diminished by time, and he can do today what nobody else can do – he can forgive and forget. We can begin again. This is not to say that what happened didn't matter, but rather that we say,

'It did matter – and now I want, by God's grace, to walk a different way.'

This can happen in marriage – we can set each other free of the past. If we are to love against the odds, we need to go on asking forgiveness of each other. I asked it of Dianne recently – asked it because of an attitude in which I suddenly realised that I had been wrong for years. How could I undo those years? I could not. But I could say to her, 'I don't take this lightly – I'm sorry: please forgive me.'

Forgiveness is liberating . . .

When my mother, who is now eighty-five, was a child, she lived in the country. Her uncle, who lived in the same house, used to lay traps for starlings before he went to bed. She would often wake herself while the dawn was just breaking and slip quietly downstairs and into the garden. And there she would find a bird caught by a wire – a creature born to fly – held to the ground. And little fingers would loose the cord and rest the bird on her hand while it grasped the fact that it was free. And then she would lift it and watch – as something that seemed to have lost all hope soared into the sky again . . .

12

Till Debt us do Part

The phone rang and a mother picked it up. It was her daughter – married just two years ago – and she was in tears. 'Mum,' she said, 'a letter has just come from the bank and I don't know how to tell John.' Her mother asked, 'Is it you who has been over-spending – you were always so careful?' 'No, it's him. But I know what will happen. He'll tell me not to worry, and then we'll row . . . and I just know I can't go on like this. They're talking about taking our house, but John will just put his head in the sand and hope it will all go away.'

It was Spike Milligan who said, 'Money can't buy you friends, but you get a better class of enemy!' If the surveys are to be believed, it's certain that financial matters have the ability to make enemies out of partners within marriage. Over seventy per cent of couples interviewed in a recent study cited rows and pressure caused by money trouble as the main cause of their break-up.[1]

If you identify with that in any way, let me say two things to you. Firstly, you are not alone; many of your friends and even family are going through similar things, but find it hard to talk about it. Secondly, this chapter won't condemn you, but it could help you on the road to getting your finances under control, having fewer rows about money, and even getting a little more sleep.

So many families are experiencing the crushing worry

that debt problems bring. Some of these families will be relatively well off, and others poor. The problem of debt is no respecter of persons. Often an image of well-being can hide a tragic situation. And we would be fools to believe that the Christian community is immune to these pressures; almost certainly you sit Sunday by Sunday near to somebody who sings all the hymns with verve, who may be involved in many church activities, seems to have a happy marriage, but is tormented by the worry of debt.

Most of us have known the feeling of hopelessness when we realise that we are just over-committed. The phrase 'can't make ends meet' says it all. The picture is of somebody trying with all their might to get things together – but there just isn't enough to go around.

If we are going to be able to love against the odds, it's almost certain that at some time in our marriage we are going to have to deal with the assault on love that comes from financial pressure.

I am involved in a debt-counselling project. At the Centre we see a tremendous variety of people who, for one reason or another, cannot cope financially. The vast majority of them are not in that situation because they have been deliberately foolish with money. That is not to say that with a little hindsight they wouldn't change some things. But the fact is that many have suffered the effects of unemployment, sickness, or simply found it hard to cope in a society which pushes the use of credit, but offers no real help in how to manage the resulting debt. I often meet people who say, 'I am always overdrawn – no matter what I do, I cannot get in control – it almost seems as if my overdraft has a life of its own!'

We all need to have a degree of humility when it comes to these issues. The problem is not just the big-spender next door – it's the family on income support who, far from draining the system, are possibly not claiming all the benefits to which they are legally entitled. It's the middle-manager suddenly hit by recession, the factory worker who has suddenly had all overtime stopped, or the career woman whose sales have suddenly plummeted. In short, it could have (and probably has!) happened to us.

The 'Victims' of Debt

With regard to money, each of us needs to bear responsibility for our actions. If we use it foolishly, we get into difficulty. Having said that, I believe that in our society there are many who have become the 'victims' of debt. One of the reasons is that people have walked into a minefield with no warning.

Nobody prepared the generations that married after the 1960s for the fact that large-scale credit was to become a major part of everyday life. Their parents may have occasionally run up a bill at the grocer's or bought a three-piece suite on hire purchase, but the whole climate of borrowing was quite different then.

There is now a concerted effort, on behalf of business interests of all sorts, to encourage people to borrow – and often to do so without careful consideration of their ability to repay.

When I first became a solicitor, building societies were prepared to grant a mortgage which equalled two or two-and-a-half times the income of the main wage earner. They would only do that, however, if the borrowers had been saving with them for a period of time and had demonstrated their ability to handle money wisely.

In the mid-Eighties all that changed. Alterations in the regulations as to how building societies, and later banks, could raise the money they lent meant there was an explosion of lending. The financial institutions were falling over themselves to get rid of funds, and they radically changed their lending criteria. Suddenly it was possible to borrow three times the joint income of a couple, and four times was not impossible. The need to have demonstrated a regular savings pattern went overnight.

But it wasn't just that borrowing money for mortgages became easier – the credit-card boom was now under way. Access ran an advertisement that said, 'Take the waiting out of wanting.' The message was, 'You deserve it, and you deserve it *now*.' Plastic cards weren't new, but this kind was different. Until the 1980s most of the plastic was in the form of 'charge cards' on which the full balance was normally repaid at the end of the month. But the new credit cards asked only that at the end of each month you repay five per cent of the outstanding balance. That may have been good news, except for the fact that the interest charged on the amount not paid was often three times that charged on a house mortgage.

We now have thirty-five million credit cards in use in this country. That compares with two million in Germany.[2] Of course, credit cards have real advantages. They are very convenient, and if you always pay the full balance off at the end of each month you actually obtain some free credit. Their real disadvantage is that if you have a credit card, you need a will of iron to resist spending more than you can afford. Surveys have shown that those who use credit cards tend to spend over a third more in a year than those who use other means.[3] That's not difficult to understand; it's so easy when we use plastic to convince ourselves that it's not real money.

But it doesn't stop there. Have you noticed that some stores won't accept your ordinary credit cards? That's normally because they want you to use their own. And the interest rates on those cards are even higher than normal bank credit cards.

Keith Tondeur, who wrote *Escape from Debt*, was shopping in one of the large department stores. The young man in front of him had just offered his credit card to pay for a compact disc player. It was rejected as being over the limit. The sales assistant then offered him one of the store cards and asked him to fill in the forms there and then. The young man obtained a credit limit and left clutching his new purchase. Keith asked the sales assistant if it were not irresponsible to offer further credit to a person who was already in difficulty. He says that the sales assistant's reply is etched into his memory: 'I don't care whether he eventually pays or not. I get commission for every store card I get a customer to take.'

Credit is thrown at us. The other day I got a letter from one of the large banks. It told me that as I was a valued customer they had set aside a loan for me at a preferential rate of twenty-six per cent! With friends like that, I have no need of enemies. The madness can be summed up in the advertisement which appeared in one of our national newspapers: 'Now you can borrow enough to get completely out of debt!'

So there it was, the brave new world of borrowing. It said you could have it all and you could have it now. You could have the house you wanted, and the car you wanted, and the gadgets you wanted, and if you got into trouble on one credit card – well, you could always pay it off by using another one. Overdrafts, second mortgages, hire purchase, holiday loans – there was no end to it.

The good news is that even if we are in the middle of financial trauma, we can learn lessons which can not only help us recover, but can keep us debt-free for life. But the key ingredient is honesty.

Being honest with each other

The reason that financial difficulty is at the heart of so much marital stress is that it has the ability to hit us at the heart of our self-esteem and then to isolate us. If we fall ill, we are prepared to accept medical help – even a little sympathy. But debt problems so often scream at us, 'You got into this mess, you get out of it; don't even tell your husband or wife.' Financial difficulty seems to have the ability to make those going through it feel as though they are the only ones who have ever experienced the long nights when you cry yourself to sleep or wake with the fear of the morning's post.

Those who are experiencing it feel a variety of emotions. Foremost may be guilt. David put it like this: 'How could I have got my family into such a mess? All I ever wanted was to give them the best – now it looks as if we'll lose everything.'

Hard on the heels of guilt is often a feeling of crushing loneliness. The temptation is to retreat to the safety of silence towards our partner, irritability towards our children or friends, and 'Oh fine' towards everyone else.

The first step is to face the issue. This may well involve us in some straight talking. It may be that one of the partners has double standards in this area. Typical would be a husband or wife moaning incessantly about some over-spending by their partner of £2.50, and then promptly going out and spending £50 on some gadget that will 'save money in the long-term'.

A wife related how she first discovered the terrible financial mess that her husband had got into:

One day I went to a cupboard that we hardly used. As I pulled open the door, a flood of unopened mail fell out. There were bills, bank statements, letters demanding money and even court summonses. I asked my husband, 'Why didn't you tell me?' He said, 'I was so ashamed – I thought that I should be able to sort it out myself. I just hoped it would go away.'

In another case, Ralph lost his job at the factory. He couldn't bring himself to tell Mary, and every day for three months he left home at the normal time. Mary had no idea that there was a problem and continued to spend as normal – until the day that the first cheque bounced.

We may find that situation hard to understand. But those who have never known it can only guess at the sense of hopelessness that can accompany the loss of a job. The loss hits at once in so many areas, not least at the heart of one's self-esteem. Crushing debt makes it hard for us to think rationally. A very common reaction is to try to ignore it; to hope that somehow the problem will just go away.

Mary put it like this: 'I had no idea of the weight that he was carrying. I went on spending as usual – but I should have realised. I suppose I just chose not to.'

A comment that we often hear is, 'I don't know where to turn.' That is so understandable, and yet somehow we have to make a move. The first step is to acknowledge the problem and talk about it to each other. That is not an easy task. It may be painful, it will often include asking for forgiveness, but it's the *only* way forward if we are to come out of the problem together.

Money talks!

Set aside a regular time each week to talk about financial matters. Do this in a place that can double up as your 'office'. It doesn't matter if it's the kitchen table, so long as nearby are all the materials that you need – outstanding bills, credit-card statements, bank statements, cheque stubs, lists of standing orders, paper clips, rubber bands, envelopes, stamps and writing paper. These are some of the weapons that you will need for this battle, but, like all wars, it helps to know as much about the enemy as possible.

Honesty about the *real* problem

One of the most basic and sobering lessons for many of us is that our financial problems are not those of too little income, but rather of too large an expenditure. For such people, the idea that financial trauma can be sorted out by a rise in income is a myth. That is not true of everybody. For some, the problem is simply income – they are too poor. What they need is not clever ideas on getting ten meals from five chicken bones – they need more income. But that is not the case with many of us.

My father was a postman and my mother a cleaner. We lived in a rented house, and life was simple to say the least. Non-essentials like heating in the bedrooms, fitted carpets, and toilet paper (don't ask!) belonged to another world. I didn't eat in a restaurant until I was sixteen. But I had everything I needed in that home, including wise advice from a father who would take me aside regularly and recite to me the words of Mr Micawber from Dickens' *David Copperfield*: 'Annual income: twenty shillings; expenditure: nineteen shillings and sixpence – result: happiness. Annual income: twenty shillings; expenditure: twenty shillings and sixpence – result: misery.' A belief in that principle meant that my father was never in debt. You may think that he paid an unacceptable price for that. He never had a holiday away from his own home, or had his own bank account, and he never did get to taste pasta – but I have never known a man so content.

When I reached adulthood, one of the first things I did was to ignore my father's advice. I did what many of us do – live just above our income, whatever that is. That's why the book of Ecclesiastes says, 'A man (or woman!) will always spend more than they get.'[4] That's why that next pay rise is never quite enough to get us out of trouble. It helps for a month or two, but soon we're back in the same situation. That's why even if we move from a large house to a small one, and for a while have some money in the bank, it's not long before the money is gone and we wonder how it happened again.

When Dianne and I were married, we had the same amount in the bank as my father – nothing. But I had other ideas. I was in the process of qualifying as a solicitor,

that the cash being spent is real money and, if it's not our own, the cost of borrowing it is high. The following table shows you just how high (these are *typical rates, and may vary as between various lenders*):

Mortgage = bank base rate + 2% per year (tax relief on first £30,000)

Overdraft = bank base rate + 12–14% per year + monthly charge (typically £5–£10)

Unauthorised overdraft = bank base rate + 20–25% per year + monthly charge (typically £12–£30)

Credit Cards (e.g., Visa, Access) = 21–25% APR*

Store cards (e.g., Dixons, Marks & Spencer) = 25%–40% APR

Unlicensed (illegal) money lenders = anything they can get away with. One borrower was charged at 400,000%!

Those who have never known the devastating effect of financial pressure can only guess at the trauma, but they should be assured that it is real. Where it exists, it affects every member of the family. The National Society for the Prevention of Cruelty to Children recently ran an advertising campaign with this warning: 'When dad falls behind with the mortgage, it's the children who end up paying.' It was a powerful reminder of just how deeply financial trauma can affect us, so that we end up lashing out – either physically or verbally – at those we love.

Sally was a young mum who didn't want to hurt her husband by telling him he just wasn't earning enough to support their family. She simply didn't have enough money to pay the rent, and she spent four months intercepting the

* APR means Annual Percentage Rate. It represents the total cost of borrowing and takes into account not only the way in which the interest is calculated but also any borrowing charges, fees and insurance premiums. It is always calculated in the same way, and so comparing APRs is a good way of comparing the cost of borrowing money from different places. By law, most lenders must quote the APR on agreements.

post so that he would never find out. That issue dominated every waking moment. The day came when the landlord offered her a way out.

No one knows what emotional state Sally was in that made her decide to sleep with a stranger in order to protect her husband. We don't condone what she did – but our hearts go out to her. Let's never forget how financial pressure can play such tricks on the mind. It swamps us with worry and causes us to forget the things which actually matter to us most of all. So often, debt robs us of dignity. We lose self-respect and come to believe that we've made such a mess of it all that we don't deserve to be loved. And then, in the darkest moment, somebody says to us, 'I will love you, and together we will come through this.'

That's the heart of loving against the odds. It means sticking by each other when times are tough. It means forgiving when someone has let us down badly. It means wanting with all our hearts to change. It's a mixture of hope, faith, love and courage. It strains its neck to look forward to better times, and holds its head from always glancing back. It says, 'It's been harder than we could have imagined – but with God's help we can love and respect again.'

13

Loving Against the Odds

A husband went to a marriage counsellor. 'In our twelve years of marriage', the husband complained, 'we haven't been able to agree on anything.' 'It's been eleven years, dear,' the wife corrected.

Even if we are not to know that level of trauma in our marriage, it's certain that we will go through periods that will test our love.

The young couple stand at the altar together. Just behind, a small boy, looking as if he's about to die at any moment, loosens the collar on his page-boy suit. A father shuffles from foot to foot, afraid that he might miss his big moment. The bride looks marvellous and the groom has had a haircut.

It could be any wedding anywhere in the country. It is a day of hope, into which is injected only one note of discord. Words are spoken which dare to question the bliss of this marriage scene. And they come at the heart of the wedding service. They are prophetic. They acknowledge the joy and the love of this day, but then they stretch our vision, and cause this couple to consider how they will react when more difficult times come. They recite, 'for richer, for poorer, for better, for worse, in sickness and in health'. It is as if the writers of the service are saying to them. 'If you are going to know love that lasts a lifetime, then at some time you will need to "love against the odds".' The difficult times hit every marriage.

Dianne and I had experienced our share of the normal troubles that hit every couple, but on a cold winter's morning, when we had been married for just over ten years, we entered a period when the warnings of the wedding service came echoing back. On that morning Dianne woke and said, 'Rob, I can't cope any more.' The words ushered in what were to become the darkest years of our life together.

It had begun two years before that winter's day.

Katie was a toddler and into everything, I was rushing around in the legal practice and also involved in many outside agendas. Life was frantic.

And then Di became pregnant. We were thrilled. It seemed that life was good for us just then. We began to plan for the new arrival. Katie had already made plain her preference as to the sex of the child, and in anticipation of a favourable result, had traded one of her dolls for a football.

Miscarriage is a strange affair. Those who have never known it tend to think it slightly less traumatic than having a tooth out. But it is, in truth, the death of a loved one. Somebody to whom you have given life is not going to make it. That somebody is part of you – emotionally, physically, even spiritually. When Di was admitted to hospital all the gynaecological beds were full, and at two in the morning we were shown into a geriatric ward. Surrounded by the soft moans of those whose lives were coming to an end, we held hands in the darkness and mourned the loss of a young life.

In our work at CARE for the Family we often come across such a situation. Often the woman involved will tell us that nobody, even family, seems to understand the sense of loss that she is experiencing. Some have had several miscarriages and known multiple grief, often coupled with the fear that they will never be able to have children. They must be allowed to mourn – they have lost a child. I believe with all my heart that we have three children: Katie, Lloyd, and one in heaven that I am longing to meet.

In the October of the following year Lloyd was born. The joy of that hinted that just maybe we were emerging from a tough time. But in the following months Di wasn't very well – she seemed listless and even allowing for the normal effects of childbirth it seemed that there was something going on in her body that was slowly dragging her down.

Shortly after climbing into bed one night, Di began to complain of pain in her side. It got worse, and soon she was crawling along the floor in agony. She was taken into hospital and within hours her gall-bladder was removed. Di came out of hospital but never really got back to full health. We spent almost two years trying to discover what was wrong. It is a wearying business trying to get to the bottom of an illness which is not easily diagnosed. We suddenly had great sympathy with the woman in the New Testament who had been ill for twelve years and spent all she had, 'yet instead of getting better . . . grew worse'.[1] As the months went on Di began to find it so hard to cope. She was at home with a demanding toddler and a new baby. Friends and family were fantastic, but the worry of not knowing what was going on in her body, coupled with a feeling of guilt that she should be 'up and about' was causing her to sink into depression. Those were the events that lay behind that cry for help that I heard on that winter's morning.

Eventually, after innumerable tests, the medics found the source of the problem – a deficiency in Di's immune system. Treatment was able to begin and she was able to adjust her lifestyle to the physical limitations of her body. But she has never forgotten how it felt to be in that fog of despair. We too easily categorise sickness into physical and emotional. We are whole people. If our body is ill it affects our mind, and vice versa.

That experience gave us a heart for those who suffer emotional trauma. I'm sorry to say that, even in our enlightened twentieth-century society, we often find it difficult to know how to respond to those who are experiencing emotional illness. Advice often ranges from, 'Pull yourself together – there's lots worse than you,' to 'Have you tried Royal Jelly?' If you break a leg, neighbours will bake a cake; but if you have anything wrong from the neck up, dig in for a relatively lonely period – and hold on hard to the few friends who hang in there with you. Each of us should have a degree of humility in this area. When we are feeling strong it's easy to seem uncaring, but we had better realise that, almost certainly, the day will come for us too, when we reach out for somebody to understand.

Lessons from the hard times

We learnt so much at that time. I cancelled many engagements, and we spent long winter evenings talking together. We asked ourselves what had gone wrong and whether we could do anything about it. As we talked, so much came out that I am convinced would have been hidden for ever without circumstances forcing us to have a period where we said no to others and gave time to each other. Dianne shared with me hurts that had lain dormant for years. I told her of disappointments that until then I had held in my heart.

But the biggest lessons were those that we learnt about ourselves. At the time I was a partner in a law firm. People came to me with their problems. I was a leader in my local church and people wanted me on their committees. They said, 'He can make things happen.' But in my home I could make so little happen. My wife was ill, two small children had needs, and night after night I fell to my knees and prayed, 'Lord, I can do *nothing* about this situation. If I have abilities they don't seem to work here; if I have money it is valueless in this situation; even if I have power in some areas of my life – I have no power here. Please help us.'

But there were deep lessons for us still to come. The

principle of learning from the hard times is summed up in the words of the Jamie Owens-Collins song:

> Is the rain falling from the sky, keeping you from singing?
> Is that tear falling from your eye, because the wind is stinging?
> Oh don't you fret now child, don't you worry. The rain's to help you grow, so don't try to hurry the storm along.
> The hard times make you strong.[2]

Discovering the power of weakness

Dianne said to me one day, 'Rob, I'm not able to go to church at the moment. Could we please open our home to others who are going through difficult times? It may be they have a crisis of faith or that life has been hard for them.' I asked her what we could give such a group. She told me that we could give them what we had – our weakness.

We met every Wednesday evening and called it 'For strugglers'. People crowded into our home – people of all kinds – doctors, the unemployed, homemakers, the rich and the poor, anyone who owned the title 'struggler'.

It was in the strugglers' group that we learnt the power of weakness. Some of us are so successful in every area of our lives that nobody can get near us. But if we can share a little of our own weakness – failure even – we set them free. At that time I went to visit a businessman who I knew was going through a hard time. I asked him, 'How are you?' He replied, 'Oh, fine. How are you?' I said, 'Not good, Di is ill, I find I'm crying more as a man than I did as a boy.' It was as if I took a cork out of a bottle and he began to share the deep issues of his life with me.

If it were not for the lessons learnt at that time – the need to listen to each other, to give each other time, and the fact that it's alright to fail, I doubt that we would be involved in the work we do now with those whose lives have been touched by pain.

Shortly after that experience I was asked to give a talk at our church about marriage, and I wrote a poem that tried to sum up our particular journey – the good times and the bad. I gave it such an original title – 'To my wife'!

I have loved you,
Loved you when we held hands feverishly,
In the back of the Gaumont cinema in Queen Street.
And I have loved you, loved you when we were married,
Loved you as we scoured junk shops, furnishing our first
    flat.
And picking up fantastic bargains (and wardrobes with
    woodworm in them!)

We built a home.
And I loved you when she was born, and
Suddenly we were three.
And then he came, and throughout all the sunshine
    and the joy, I have loved you.

And I have loved you in the darkness, when we cried
    together.
And the tunnel seemed so very long and so very black.
And you loved me, with all my inconsistency and
    hypocrisy,
When all the great hopes came so often to so little, went
    on loving.

And we have loved each other, you and I.
Loved when at times it seemed that love had died,
And all there was – was just the hope that it would grow
    again.
Come fighting, kicking through the frost.
And it did, came stronger, purer, finer, truer.
And today it is Saturday, and today I can say,
I have loved you.

It was not many years later that I was going through such a difficult time myself and it was Dianne's arms around me.

I can remember a vicar saying to me after one of our seminars for church leaders, 'I was so afraid that you would just come with clever answers. Thank you for sharing a little of your own difficulty with us.' Each of us go through difficult times in our marriage. It may be finance, or the fact that love seems to have died and everything yells out, 'Let go – it's over.' It may be that illness or redundancy puts our marriage under incredible pressure. These are trying circumstances. It would be foolish to minimise them. But issues like these are common to every marriage, and if we are to go on loving then at some time we will need to love against the odds.

It is also true that we learn lessons in those hard times that can change us for ever. Cathy and Tony wrote to me about the lessons learnt in such a time in their marriage:

We had been married for eighteen years and had three lovely children. My husband is an insurance broker, I am a nurse. Life was at times a little over-busy, but we were so happy. Then one day my son Jack, aged eight, went down with a bug. He was ill for a while but we put it down to a typical child's illness. However, it went on and on and eventually we saw a consultant. He decided to do a brain scan which revealed a brain tumour. Our son had terminal cancer.

One of the main lessons we learnt when Jack became ill was how important it is to talk openly as a family. At that time the girls were thirteen and ten. We didn't find it easy to talk, but we started a little family ritual to help us. Every Sunday evening we would light a candle and put it in the middle of the room (Jack would light this). Then we would each say how we felt. We could share anything at all, and when anybody was speaking nobody else could interrupt. We could all comment later, but we tried not to be critical. My teenage daughter found it so hard at first, but soon we were all sharing how we felt. We found that we could talk about all sorts of things and didn't really need the candle, but it was a way of getting us together to talk.

Tony and I learnt not only to tell Jack how much we loved him, but to tell him how much we loved each other. He died shortly after a major operation. His last words to me were, 'I love you,' and on his gravestone we put: 'Faith hope and love ... but the greatest of these is love.'

When I read that I cried. But mixed with the sadness was the joy that this little family had somehow learnt to love each other in a deeper way, not because of easy times, but against the odds.

Love without conditions

In his book *Mortal Lessons: Notes in the Art of Surgery*, Richard Seltzer, a surgeon, recounts the following incident:

I stand by the bed where a young woman lies, her face post-operative, her mouth twisted in palsy, clownish. A tiny twig of the facial nerve, the one to the muscles of her mouth has been severed. She will be thus from now on. The surgeon has followed with religious fervour, the curve of her flesh, I promise you that. Nevertheless, to remove the tumour in her cheek, I have cut a little nerve. Her young husband is in the room. He stands on the opposite side of the bed and together they seem to dwell in the evening lamp light, isolated from me, private. 'Who are they?', I ask myself, 'He and this wry mouth that I have made. Who gaze at and touch each other so greedily.' The young woman speaks. 'Will my mouth always be like this?' she asks. 'Yes it will,' I say. 'It is because the nerve was cut.' She nods and is silent, but the young man smiles, 'I like it,' he says, 'it's kind of cute.' And all at once, I know who he is and I lower my gaze. One is not bold in an encounter with a god. And unmindful I see he bends to kiss her crooked mouth, and I so close, I can see how he twists his own lips to accommodate to hers, to show their kiss still works. And I remember that the gods appeared in ancient times as mortals and I hold my breath, and let the wonder in.[3]

I remember reading that at a seminar, and a woman of about sixty coming up to me. She had obviously just been crying. As she smiled at me I noticed a slight disfigurement to the side of her mouth. She said, 'Rob, my mouth used to be much worse than this, but only as you read that passage, I realised that for twenty years my husband has been altering the shape of his lips to prove our kiss still works.'

These are not lessons that are learnt in the easy times. They are born out of pain. In fact what her husband did was a parable of all our marriages. There comes a time for most of us when our partner becomes unattractive to us for a while. It may be physically, mentally, emotionally, or intellectually. At such a time love does not rise easily in our hearts. It is rather that from the very depths of our spirits, almost as an act of the will, we love against the odds. In short, we are altering the shape of *our* lips to prove the kiss still works.

The essence of this is unconditional love – something that many of us find hard to give. We are used to loving those who meet our needs, or who think as we do, or who fulfil some ego need in us. But few have ever experienced love which has no strings and no demands. Even from parents many have only known a love that gives the impression that it is dependent on achievement.

I remember Katie coming home from school some years ago. She came bursting through the door and said, 'I got ninety-five per cent in maths, dad!' I had two questions for that little girl – 'What happened to the five per cent?' and 'Where were you in the class order?' I'm ashamed of that now. It seems that today we are putting weights on our children's shoulders they are not strong enough to bear.

It is a wearying business having to earn love. I regularly meet adults, especially men, who are still desperately trying to prove themselves to their father. These people may be successful in their jobs and careers, and others may look at them and wish they could be like them. But they crave the approval of their father. Such people find it hard to love against the odds in marriage – even for a short time. They have been taught that love is earned.

If we are to love against the odds in marriage, then at times we are going to have to love when our needs are not being met, and when we don't *feel* like loving, and without strings.

The challenge of change

Does unconditional love mean that we abandon the hope of change? Does it mean that we forgo the right to say to our partner, 'I wish that you would change in this area or that'? No, on the contrary it means that we face the need for change in each other and deal with it. God loves us unconditionally, but he has great plans to change us. There are three indispensable keys to unlocking the door of change.

Accept what you can't change
When I was a boy of fifteen I was no better at do-it-yourself than I am now. That wouldn't have mattered, save for the prospect of the woodwork examination. The teacher told us that we had a choice: we could either make a coffee table or a potato plunger. For the uninitiated, a potato

plunger is rather like a mallet with a pointed end. It's hard to remember if anybody in Form 4b had the slightest inclination to plant potatoes, but if we had, then apparently this tool was indispensable. You thrust it into the ground to make way for the potato.

I gave the construction of that implement everything I had. I practically prayed over it. Finally it was finished. I laid it on my desk and awaited the inspection. The teacher, after having practically given Charles Harries the Nobel Peace Prize for his coffee table, turned to me. He glanced at the collection of wood on my desk and asked, 'What is it?' I thought that was rather hard – it obviously wasn't the coffee table. 'Sir,' I said, 'it's a potato plunger.' He said, 'It's awful!' I mumbled, 'I did my best.' And that was when he said something as a result of which he nearly tasted the potato plunger, and which I have never forgotten. He said, 'Parsons, your best is not good enough.'

I have often thought about that. Where do you go as a boy of fifteen if your best isn't good enough?

It's true of some of our marriages. We try hard to change our partners into somebody they cannot be. Peter Sellers' fourth wife said that shortly before he died he would wake in the night, consumed with the question of his own identity. Do you ever wonder who you are, perhaps asking 'Will the real me please stand up?'

We all wear many masks during the day. But it's tragic if we have to go on wearing them in the home. It may be that a wife feels the pressure always to look immaculate, or be the perfect church leader's wife, or that a husband has to pretend to be in total control when really he wants to cry and be held. I thank God that I come home to a woman who knows the very worst about me, and has decided to love me anyway.

This is not to say that change is a bad thing. We all want our partners to change; we want our bosses or workmates to change. Change is good, it is dynamic. Having said that, where one partner tries to make the other into somebody they cannot be, then love dies.

This is also true of our children. The day is seared into my memory. It was my daughter Katie's school sports day. As I wandered across the field my mind had gone back to my own childhood and the catalogue of sporting achievements I had managed to log up – 400 yards, fourth; 200 yards, fifth (and so on!). As I waited for the start of the 100 yards for 2A, I sensed in my mind that my child was about to wipe out a generation of failure. I had somehow pushed to the back of my mind the fact that, although my little girl was already a budding poet, she was no athlete.

An excited buzz went around the crowd. Video cameras were lifted, mothers fumbled for handkerchiefs and elastoplast. They were off!

After a while I realised, to my utter amazement, that Katie was out in front – and she stayed there. Well almost. When she was about ten yards from the line, I yelled: 'Go for it Katie!' Whereupon she stopped, turned, waved, and said, 'Hello daddy!' – and the whole of 2A swept by. Of course, I was frustrated, especially as the father next to me (whose child is always Mary in the nativity play, and was reading Dickens shortly after birth), was grinning – again!

But that frustration is nothing compared to the trauma I'm going to have to face unless I learn that you cannot always make people into what you want them to be. God has given each of us not only unique fingerprints, but individual gifts and limitations. We need the space and encouragement from those who love us to become the man or woman we are meant to be.

Change can be a frustrating thing. One of the problems with it is that so often we want people to change into our view of perfection. That is the opposite of loving against the odds. A long-term bachelor had decided that he was going to get married. He had read how hard it is to change people after marriage, so he sent the dating agency a very clear description of the kind of woman he was looking for: 'I want a companion who is small, attractive, loves water sports and enjoys group activities.' He eagerly waited for the letter containing his first introduction. The computer answered, 'Marry a penguin.'

Let your partner know your hopes for change!

One of the most common mistakes when a marriage hits a rocky patch is for the couple to put their heads in the sand and say, 'Things will improve – just give it time.' The sombre truth of the statistics is that for many couples things do not improve. It's vital at the first sign of difficulty in the marriage to talk about it and take it seriously enough to do something about it. We need to let our partners know how we feel about issues, including change in how we relate to each other.

A friend of mine was counselling a couple about a divorce after fifteen years of marriage. He asked the wife, 'Why are you leaving him?' She replied, 'When he behaves in a certain way – I hate it. I can't take any more.' The counsellor asked, 'Have you ever told him that?' 'No, I've never told him.' He turned to the husband, 'Did you have any idea about this?' 'No, I never knew she felt like that.' They had been married for fifteen years, were about to split up, and hadn't had the most basic communication about what was destroying their love.

In another case a couple at the very door of the divorce court began to talk about the possibility of saving their marriage. 'What can I do to change?' he said. He was expecting something profound. What he got was: 'I want you to hold me without it leading to sex every time. I want you to compliment me in front of other people and say that you love me. I want you, some nights, to let the phone ring when I am talking to you. I want you to make me feel as if you want me.' That was thirteen years ago. They are still married, still love each other, and are still changing.

When you can't change your partner – change yourself!

One of the greatest barriers to rediscovering love in a marriage is where one of the partners comes to believe that their partner will never change and 'there's no point in hoping'.

The incredible thing is, even if our partner can't or won't change, *we can change*. And, because change is dynamic, it affects everybody it comes into contact with. Change breeds change. It may be hard to alter our partner, but we can sometimes change ourselves. One husband put it like this:

> For years I had wanted my wife to be a certain kind of person. I looked at other men's wives and wished she could be like that. One night I was in the pub and my friend told me that his marriage was breaking up. He said 'You don't know what it's like living with Sue. I wish she was like your Sally.' I thought, 'My Sally – he wants her to be like *my wife*.' At that moment I ripped up the piece of paper on which I had scribbled all I wanted my wife to be. I suddenly saw the beauty of all that she was. I know it sounds daft – but it was like falling in love again. Sally is the same – but I changed!

There is sometimes another problem to do with change. It is not that our partner won't change, but rather that we won't let them change. We expect them never to change. We don't allow for physical, emotional and even spiritual change. Laurie Peak put it well, 'A woman marries a man with the ridiculous belief that she can change him. A man marries a woman with the naïve idea that she will continue to be the same.'

The love of two people is never a simple thing. It is capable of bringing out the highest virtues of a man or a woman, and within moments the most despicable traits. We do often hurt most the ones we love best of all. But it is not meant to be so.

I sometimes wonder why that lovely definition of love found in 1 Corinthians 13 is so often only read at wedding services. What if we were to sit with our partner and ask each other, 'What does it mean for us to love like that?'

Love is patient, love is kind. It does not envy, it does not boast, it is not proud. It is not rude, it is not self-seeking, it is not easily angered, it keeps no record of wrongs. Love does not delight in evil but rejoices with the truth. It always protects, always trusts, always hopes, always perseveres.

Love never fails.[4]

What if we were to ask each other, 'What does it mean for you and me that "love is kind", or that "it keeps no record of wrongs"?' What can it mean that 'love is patient', 'not self-seeking' and 'not easily angered'? And what can it possibly mean that 'love never fails'? In short, what does it mean to love against the odds?

This is how one wife summed all of that up:

I took you love.
In sickness or in health,
For better or for worse.
And now I live my promise out.

Charmed with each other's youth,
We could not know
That someday you would drool
And shuffle and forget your words
While I would keep
My warmth and wit and swiftness.
I use them now to cherish you.
To wrap you round with gentleness
And patient courtesy.

I love you dear
All the goods you have been to me

215

Still halo you.
The promises we made
Hold and support us both.
We are each other's cross,
Each other's greatest blessing.[5]

Sometimes it's hard to know where to start in all this. Our heads and hearts are swimming with so many emotions. Some of you are, at this very moment, experiencing such difficult times. But if you want to save your love, if you believe that you could find again what you have lost, then you have to begin down that road. What is certain is that such a beginning cannot just be in the mind or even the heart. If things are to change something must *happen*. That something can be very small. It may be an expression of appreciation instead of the expected criticism, it may be the cancelling of some other commitment to give time to talk, it could be a touch . . .

I can almost hear some of you say, 'How naïve, to believe that a marriage that is dying can be saved by such small things.' But I promise you – they sometimes can. One man described it to me like this:

My wife and I were having a divorce. We were living apart and somehow ended up at the same party. When all the other guests were gone I looked across the room and saw that she was still there. She had to pass me to get out. As we passed we touched. I know it sounds crazy, we are a sophisticated couple, we were halfway through a divorce, but that touch did it. It somehow created in us a desire to try again. That was eight years ago. We love each other more than ever.

That beginning is vital. Whether it's a father determined to spend more time with his family, or a wife resolving to help her husband articulate all that he is bottling up inside, we have to begin. It will normally involve us in a battle on at least two fronts. Firstly, because such times will often be when the feeling of love is low, they will only happen by an act of the *will*. If we wait until we feel like taking that first step, we'll normally wait a long time. Secondly, such action will inevitably involve us in a battle with that great enemy time. It would be easier to deal with problems of relationships if we could do so in a vacuum. But we can't do that. We have to tackle them in the real world, where children have dental appointments, and the car breaks down, and a hundred people scream at us, 'Can you do this please?' But we must remember that we are fighting for the survival of love.

When Lloyd was four years old we were on a beach and he noticed some people water-skiing. He looked up at me and asked, 'Can I water-ski, dad?' I said, 'Son, you can't even swim!' He said, 'I know, but I'd like to try.'

I asked the instructor if he could help. He was kind. He offered to sit Lloyd on a wide board and give him a little ride around the bay. He put two huge safety rings around him. We could just about see Lloyd's head and feet protruding from the ends. My son sat on the board and the boat pulled him out.

When he was fifty yards out he stood and began skiing! The instructor turned to me in anger and said, 'Did you tell him to stand?' I said, 'No, I thought you must have.' My son skied all around the bay. But as he neared the end of his adventure, for no apparent reason he suddenly fell off. When he got to the beach I asked him why he had fallen like that. He said, 'Dad, I wanted to do it just like you!'

I have often wondered what made that little boy suddenly decide to stand. Somewhere in the middle of that ocean that child thought to himself, 'I think I could just . . . stand. I think I could begin.'

Beginning is never easy, and neither is loving against the odds. But it is vital that we at least try, even if the task seems so very great.

The story is told of an eastern emperor who asked his gardener to make for him a garden such as had never been seen before. The old man worked tirelessly for twenty years. Finally he said to the emperor, 'Come, walk with me in the garden that I have made for you.' They began to walk as the sun came up, and at sunset the emperor gave his verdict, 'To my eye all is well, save for one thing. I would like a row of cedar trees from the palace door to the golden gate.' The old gardener protested, 'But your majesty, a row of cedar trees from the palace door to the golden gate would take a thousand years!' 'Then', said the emperor, 'we must begin this very day. We haven't a moment to lose!'

Notes

2. Whatever Happened to Conversation?

1. P. Zimbardo, *Psychology Today*, August 1980, pp. 71–6.
2. I. MacKinnon, 'Suicide Figures are Tip of Iceberg', *The Independent*, 16 May 1992.
3. *Marriage Partnership*, Winter 1992.
4. C. and B. Snyder, *Incompatibility: Grounds for a Great Marriage* (Sisters, OR: Quester Publishers Inc., 1988), p. 62.

3. Time for Love

1. C.H. Godefroy and J. Clark, *The Complete Time Management System* (London: Judy Piatkus, 1990).
2. Robert Herrick, 'To the Virgins, To Make Much of Time', in A. Quiller-Couch (ed.), *The Oxford Book of English Verse, 1250–1918* (Oxford: Oxford University Press, 1939), p. 274.
3. Romans 12:3, J.B. Phillips translation.
4. Michael Quoist, 'Lord I Have Time', *Prayers for Life* (Dublin: Gill & Macmillan, 1963), pp. 76–8. Used with permission.

4. A Word to Fathers

1. U. Bronfenbrenner, 'The Origins of Alienation', *Scientific American*, August 1974.
2. Ephesians 5:16, paraphrased.
3. Proverbs 22:6.
4. Harry Chapin, 'Cat's in the Cradle'. Copyright 1974 by Story Songs Ltd. Used with permission.
5. P. Williams, J. Williams, and J. Jenkins, *Keep the Home Fires Glowing* (New Jersey: Fleming H. Revell, 1986), pp. 49–50.
6. Previously unpublished poem, written by Susan Ashdown. Used with permission.

5. Hey – Look Who's Talking!

1. James 1:19.
2. For a detailed treatment of word pictures, see Gary Smalley and John Trent, *The Language of Love* (California: Focus on the Family, 1988).

6. How to Fight a Good Fight

1. Ephesians 4:26.
2. D. Boorstin, *The Image* (New York: Atheneum, 1961), pp. 72–3.
3. Proverbs 17:14.
4. 1 Corinthians 13:5.
5. Psalm 130:3.
6. R. Erdoes, AD 1000, *Living on the Brink of Apocalypse* (San Francisco: Harper & Row, 1988).

7. Rain in the Desert – The Power of Appreciation

1. James Dobson, *Man to Man About Women* (Eastbourne: Kingsway, 1988).
2. K. Blanchard, *The One Minute Manager* (London: HarperCollins, 1983).
3. Marjorie Holmes, 'I Don't Feel Loved Any More', *I've Got to Talk to Somebody, God* (London: Hodder & Stoughton, 1968), pp. 18–19. Used with permission.
4. James 3:5.
5. Proverbs 17:22.
6. Mark 1:40–5.
7. F. B. Dressler, 'The Psychology of Touch', *American Journal of Psychology* 6 (1984), p. 316.
8. Ecclesiastes 7:10.
9. John 15:13.
10. Patricia McGerr, 'Johnny Lingo and the Eight-Cow Wife'. Originally published in *Woman's Day*, November 1965. Reprinted with permission from *Reader's Digest*, April 1988.

8. Rediscovering Sex

1. W. Trobisch, *The Complete Works of Walter Trobisch* (Downers Grove, IL: IVP, 1987).
2. Genesis 1:27.
3. Genesis 2:23–4.
4. Genesis 2:25.

9. Fatal Attraction

1. 1 Corinthians 10:12, RAV.
2. 'Family Policy Briefing: The Facts of Life', *Relate* 1990.
3. ibid.
4. V. Kraushaar, 'That's the Way Life Goes Sometimes',

taken from *American Girl* magazine, copyright Girl Scouts of the United States of America. Reprinted with permission.
5. Alfred Lord Tennyson, *The Works of Alfred Lord Tennyson Poet Laureate* (London: Macmillan & Co., 1905), p. 222.

10. The Heart of the Affair

1. J. Dobson, *Straight Talk to Men and Their Wives* (Dallas: Word Books, 1980), pp. 93–4. Used with permission.
2. Ella Wheeler Wilcox, 'An Unfaithful Wife to Her Husband', in Charles Mylander, *Running the Red Lights* (Ventura, CA: Regal Books, 1986), pp. 30–2. Used with permission.
3. Ephesians 5:25.
4. H. Still, *Man-Made Men* (New York: Hawthorn Books, 1973), pp. 178–9.
5. 1 Samuel 13:14.
6. 2 Samuel 11:1–5.
7. Luke 4:1–13.
8. Galatians 6:2.
9. 1 Kings 19:4.
10. Matthew 5:27–30.

11. Dealing with the Past – The Freedom of Forgiveness

1. P.F. Armstrong, 'The Surgeon's New Clothes', *Citizen* 5.2, March–April 1993.
2. Matthew 27:46.
3. Luke 23:34.
4. Matthew 6:12, paraphrased.
5. Luke 7:36–50.
6. A. Hart, *Overcoming Anxiety* (Dallas: Word, 1989). Used with permission.

7. John 8:3–11.
8. Luke 23:42–3.

12. Till Debt us do Part

1. K. Tondeur, *Escape from Debt* (London: Evangelical Alliance and Credit Action, 1993).
2. The Economics Policy Group for the Movement of Christian Democracy, *Escaping the Debt Trap* (Ware, Herts.: Christian Democrat Press, 1993).
3. ibid.
4. Ecclesiastes 5:10, paraphrased.
5. *Income-Related Benefits Estimate of Take-Up in 1989* (London: DSS, 1993); V. Fry and G. Stark, *Take-Up of Means Tested Benefit, 1984–90* (London: Rowntree and Institute of Fiscal Studies, 1993).

13. Loving Against the Odds

1. Mark 5:21–34.
2. Jamie Owens-Collins, 'Hard Times'. Published by Communique Music, USA. Used with permission.
3. R. Seltzer, *Mortal Lessons: Notes in the Art of Surgery* (New York: Simon & Schuster, 1976), pp. 45–6. Used with permission.
4. 1 Corinthians 13:4–8.
5. E. Rooney, 'Holy Matrimony', in *Marriage Partnership*, January–February 1988, p. 12.